LIGHT UPON THE WORD

LIGHT UPON THE WORD

An Anthology of Evangelical Spiritual Writings

Selected and Introduced by
HERBERT F. STEVENSON

Fleming H. Revell Company
Old Tappan, New Jersey

Library of Congress Cataloging in Publication Data
Main entry under title

Light upon the Word.

    Includes index.
    1. Evangelicalism—Addresses, essays, lectures.
    2. Christian life—Addresses, essays, lectures.
I. Stevenson, Herbert F.
BR1640.A25L54   230   79-23879
ISBN 0-8007-1105-X

CONTENTS

ACKNOWLEDGEMENTS

Extract from *The Way of Holiness* by F. B. Meyer used by permission from Marshall, Morgan & Scott Publications Ltd.

Extract from *The Way to Pentecost* by Samuel Chadwick. Used by permission from Hodder & Stoughton.

Excerpts from *The Way of Holiness* by Commissioner Samuel Brengle used by permission from the Salvation Army.

Excerpt from *The Crises of the Christ* by G. Campbell Morgan. © 1936 by Fleming H. Revell Company. Used by permission.

Excerpt from *The Divine Conquest* by A. W. Tozer. © 1950 by Fleming H. Revell Company. Used by permission.

Extracts from *Studies in the Sermon on the Mount* by D. Martyn Lloyd-Jones used by permission from Inter-Varsity Press (UK edition) and William B. Eardmans Publishing Company (US edition).

Extracts from *Christ the Controversialist* by John R. W. Stott used by permission from Inter-Varsity Press.

LIGHT UPON THE WORD

INTRODUCTION

It has been said that the Evangelical Awakening of the eighteenth century, in which John Wesley and George Whitefield were the leading figures, through its profound effect upon the poorer people of the nation averted an uprising in England comparable to that of the French Revolution across the channel. Be that as it may, the Awakening had an indisputable effect upon the religious life and thought of Britain, which endures to our own day. Faith was revitalized; doctrinal issues were precipitated and clarified—and a Calvinist versus Arminian controversy re-opened which has persisted through two centuries, and even been intensified in recent years.

The brothers John and Charles Wesley, who were senior to George Whitefield, welcomed him to the 'Holy Club' at Oxford, which is regarded as the seed-bed of Methodism. George Whitefield experienced an evangelical conversion; and after graduation all three were ordained. In 1738 Whitefield, at the invitation of the Wesleys, went to join them in Georgia, where they had gone to work among the British settlers; but the Wesleys had left, disillusioned, by the time he arrived. The visit, however, opened for Whitefield a major sphere of his life-work, in America. On his return home he found that the Wesleys had, through the Moravian Brethren, entered into the experience of salvation through faith. All three flung themselves zealously into the work of evangelism. Finding church doors closed, however, to such fervent—though ordained—preachers, George Whitefield began to preach in the open air, and urged the Wesleys to follow his example. At first they hesitated, loyal churchmen as they were, until the constraint to reach the masses overcame their inhibitions, and the open fields became the principal scene of the Awakening, as crowds of many thousands listened eagerly to the Gospel.

Unhappily a rift in their relationship occurred, as doctrinal differences became apparent in their preaching. John Wesley, an Arminian, emphasized the responsibility of individuals, endowed with free will, to respond to the Gospel, and to continue in 'abiding' relationship with the Lord. George Whitefield, a Calvinist, stressed the doctrines of predestination and the perseverance of the saints. Those elected to salvation would be saved, and were secure for time

and eternity. Wesley considered this to be dangerous teaching —
indeed, antinomianism. He thought it implied that, once saved, the
'elect' could live as they liked; they could never perish, however much
they might dishonour their profession. He insisted upon the necessity
for continuing faith and obedience, every day and all the days until
life's end. He also taught the possibility of perfection through the
eradication of the sinful human nature — which Whitefield refuted.

This breach led to a controversy between Wesley and Whitefield,
which was taken up even more fiercely by their followers. The two
streams of teaching characterize Evangelical spiritual writings from
their generation until our own. In this book we have eschewed the
polemical literature which abounded in the eighteenth century,
except for allowing the two principals to state their case. Wesley's
sermon on Predestination presents his view of this great theme, while
Whitefield's letters make clear his interpretation of the matter — and
also show the sad effects of the controversy, in the spoiling of their
relationship with one another, as well as in its impact upon their
converts. While avoiding the dispute so far as possible, however,
echoes of it are inevitably found in some of our excerpts.

That such a spiritual revival should have been attended by
discordant disputation was tragic: its continuing entail is no less sad.
Happily it is not essential to take sides, and while some ardent advocates of both extremes still criticize and denounce one another, the
majority of Evangelicals have held to a middle course — perhaps
inclining to one view or the other, but recognizing a measure of truth
in both, and firmly adhering to the fundamentals of the Gospel of
grace without emphasis on debatable doctrines.

Such was Henry Venn, himself a Calvinist, who — according to his
grandson and biographer — 'did not enforce upon the conscience of
others those particular views which he had himself imbibed. . . . He
dreaded men hastily adopting Calvinist views, and when once asked,
respecting a young minister, whether he was a Calvinist or Arminian,
he replied, "I really do not know: he is a sincere disciple of the Lord
Jesus Christ: and that is of infinitely more importance than his being
a disciple of Calvin or Arminius".'

Similar sentiments animated Philip Doddridge, who was
associated with Wesley and Whitefield in the early phase of their
great enterprise. 'He adhered to a modified Calvinism . . . but to
Arminians and thoroughgoing Calvinists alike he appeared a
trimmer.' His book *The Rise and Progress of Religion in the Soul*, is
nevertheless 'shot through with evangelical fervour . . .' as exem-
plified in the excerpt quoted. John Newton, a Calvinist, also shunned

extremism. Wesley's most ardent advocate was John Fletcher (of Madeley), though in characteristically eirenical fashion. In response, initially, to provocative statements by Walter Shirley, an aggressive Calvinist, Fletcher issued five 'Checks Against Antinomianism'. We turn, however, to his 'Six Spiritual Letters', found in his desk after his death, for a 'writing' exemplifying that saintliness of character which made him so greatly and widely beloved. Incidentally, among Whitefield's chief protagonists were Sir Richard Hill, in whose family John Fletcher had once been tutor; his brother Rowland Hill; and Augustus Toplady.

There is a gap in outstanding writings after Fletcher and John Newton until the nineteenth century; then, with an excerpt from Andrew Bonar we look north of the border, to the rich spiritual heritage of Scottish presbyterianism. A staunch Calvinism derived, not from the Evangelical Awakening, but further back, from the Reformers and Covenanters, marks their entire thought; but their literature joins the twofold stream from the Awakening, in the make-up of Britain's Evangelical heritage. Robert Murray McCheyne is a shining example of fervent Scottish pastoral solicitude for the 'flock' committed to the trust of ministers. Two other Scotsmen, Alexander Whyte and James Stalker, are representative of an array of scholar-preachers who adorn the religious history of their race. Andrew Murray and W. Graham Scroggie were of Scottish extraction.

Wesley and Whitefield, Anglican clergymen, were driven into forming 'nonconforming' communities by the resistance of their church to their ministry and its effects. Happily the eighteenth-century prejudices of the establishment eventually faded, and distinguished churchmen, such as Bishops J. C. Ryle and Handley C. G. Moule; Prebendary H. W. Webb-Peploe and the Revs Evan Hopkins and John R. W. Stott, have gladly acknowledged themselves debtors to the Awakening. The twofold stream, however, is still distinguishable in the Arminian writings of Samuel Chadwick and Commissioner Samuel Logan Brengle — representing respectively the Wesleyan and Salvation Army teaching of Christian perfection — and the Calvinist convictions of Charles Haddon Spurgeon and Dr D. Martyn Lloyd-Jones.

A century after the Awakening, a further spiritual leap forward came with the movement from which the Keswick Convention was initiated. The most stirring religious impact on the nation since the Awakening was that effected by the evangelistic mission conducted by Dwight L. Moody and his soloist, Ira D. Sankey. In its wake, however, followed a consciousness among many ardent Evangelicals

of aridity in personal spiritual experience and lack of power in
Christian service. To them, the 'higher life' teaching emanating from
America seemed to open up new vistas of 'life abundant' in Christ.
Meetings held in London in 1874, and conferences at Oxford and
Brighton, inspired the arranging of the first Convention at Keswick,
in Cumberland, in July 1875. In annual gatherings ever since, except
during the two world wars, the 'Keswick' teaching of victory over sin
and power in service through the indwelling Holy Spirit has been
proclaimed.

Leaders of this new movement included Evan H. Hopkins—its
most influential personality and speaker—and W. H. Webb-Peploe.
Hopkins' authoritative book, *The Law of Liberty in the Spiritual
Life*, defined once and for all the main stream of Keswick teaching.
Webb-Peploe's address on 'Sin in the Believer' similarly provided the
opening key-note in the sequence of Convention ministry. Handley
Moule, F. B. Meyer, Campbell Morgan, and W. Graham Scroggie
frequently spoke at Keswick; as do G. B. Duncan and J. R. W. Scott.

Something of the interplay of revival movements in Britain and
America, beginning with the Awakening, is hinted at in our excerpts; but the subject is too vast to touch upon here. Our British
literary storehouse has been avidly explored by American readers;
and the Atlantic has proved no barrier to the exchange of thoughts,
experiences, and preachers. American Evangelicalism is deeply
indebted to the twofold stream flowing from the Evangelical
Awakening, and it is fitting that we should include excerpts from the
writings of two of their own most widely esteemed authors. Commissioner Brengle and Dr A. W. Tozer were both exponents of
Wesley's doctrine, and their writings are still exercising considerable
influence in Britain as well as in their own country.

The predominant theme of Evangelical spiritual writings, it will be
clear, is the relationship to God of individual Christians—a
relationship begun in conversion 'by grace through faith'; and the
cultivation of that relationship in communion with God through
Bible reading and prayer. Key-phrases are 'abiding in Christ', and
'walking with the Lord'. Mysticism, as fostered in the Catholic and
Orthodox traditions, is largely absent from Evangelical literature
(though see the contributions by Andrew Murray and Charles
Haddon Spurgeon). An intensely practical note characterizes it: the
promotion of holiness of character and conduct, issuing from
'abiding' fellowship with God.

*   *   *

It would be remiss in such a book as this not to mention the literary heritage in verse, particularly in hymns, flowing from the Evangelical Awakening. Beginning with Philip Doddridge, several of our authors were also notable hymn-writers; outstanding among them, of course, was Charles Wesley, whose contribution to the Awakening was second only to that of his brother John, though overshadowed by it. So abundant is the wealth of hymnody that it would be impossible, through space limitations, to include even a selection in this volume.

*   *   *

This book's distinctive character was suggested by Mr David Winter: my part has been to carry his conception into effect. Invaluable 'pointers' to suitable authors and excerpts have been made by several friends of differing schools of thought, especially the Revs Dr A. Skevington Wood, Dr D. Martyn Lloyd-Jones, and Dr John Stott; but responsibility for the choice of excerpts has been entirely mine. Few people, probably, will wholly agree with my selection; it may well be asked why I have omitted this or that renowned author, and why I have not included this or that superb passage. The guiding principles of my choice have been: (1) that selected excerpts should stand upon their own feet — *i.e.*, be complete in themselves, and not refer back and forth to other parts of the book from which they are taken; (2) that subjects should be varied, reflecting the wide range of Evangelical spiritual writings; and (3) that they should be of moderate length, permitting the inclusion of as many excerpts as possible.

A number of the selected items are reported addresses, and so are hortatory in style. Scripture quotations are taken, in the earlier selections, from the authorized (King James) Version; a few from the Revised Version of 1911; and latterly from the Revised Standard Version. Several of the authors take liberties, however, with the versions they quote, and adapt them to enforce their point: I have made no attempt to 'correct' them — except their wrong references! I have exercised editorial prerogative in moderating their excessive use of initial capitals and of punctuation; but their occasional idiosyncratic spelling I have left unaltered.

For the biographical notes prefacing the excerpts I am deeply indebted to the *International Dictionary of the Christian Church* (Paternoster Press) and to the American *Who Was Who in Church History*. Finally, my thanks are due to the Evangelical Library, and to the Librarian, Mr Gordon Sayer, without whose helpfulness in placing the requisite volumes at my disposal, for research and photocopying, this book could not have been produced. Above all, and as always, my wife has been my beloved companion, counsellor, and helpmeet in all that pertains to the preparation of this book.

PHILIP DODDRIDGE (1702-1751)

The youngest of 20 children — all of whom except himself and a sister died in infancy — Philip Doddridge was of frail constitution throughout his life, and died of tuberculosis in Lisbon in his fiftieth year. Orphaned at 13, friends provided for his care and education, and secured his admission to the Dissenters' Academy at Kibworth, near Leicester, in about 1723. Here he became a teacher, and pastor of the Kibworth Congregational Church. In 1729 he moved to Market Harborough, where he started his academy; and later that year was called to the church at Northampton, where he accomplished his major life-work, training students for the Nonconformist ministry, and encouraging village preaching. A man of deep piety, he is best remembered for his hymns — which were written, not for publication, but for use after his sermon in Castle Hill Church, Northampton; but his book, *The Rise and Progress of Religion in the Soul*, has been described as 'the last great Puritan spiritual autobiography'. The chapter on 'The Difficulties that Attend Religion' is of perennial spiritual applicability and appeal.

THE DIFFICULTIES THAT ATTEND RELIGION

With the utmost propriety has our divine Master required us to strive to enter in at the strait gate, thereby, as it seems, intimating, not only that the passage is narrow, but that it is beset with enemies; beset on the right hand, and on the left, with enemies cunning and formidable. And be assured, O reader, that whatever your circumstances in life are, you must meet and encounter them. It will therefore be your prudence to survey them attentively in your own reflections, that you may see what you are to expect, and may consider in what armour it is necessary you should be clothed, and with what weapons you must be furnished to manage the contest. You have often heard them marshalled, as it were, under three great leaders, the flesh, the world, and the devil; and according to this distribution, I would call you to consider the forces of each, as setting themselves in array against you. O that you may be excited to take to yourself the whole armour of God, and to acquit yourself like a man, and a Christian.

Let your conscience answer, whether you do not carry about with you a corrupt and degenerate nature? You will, I doubt not, feel its effects. You will feel, in the language of the apostle (who speaks of it as the case of Christians themselves), the flesh lusting against the Spirit, so that you will not be able, in all instances, to do the things that you would. You brought irregular propensities into the world along with you; and you have so often indulged those sinful inclinations that you have greatly increased their strength; and you will find, in consequence of it, that these habits cannot be broke through without great difficulty. You will, no doubt, often recollect the strong figures in which the prophet describes a case like yours; and you will own that it is justly represented by that of an Ethiopian changing his skin, and the leopard his spots.

It is indeed possible that you may find such an edge and eagerness upon your spirit as may lead you to imagine that all opposition will immediately fall before you. But alas! I fear that in a little time these enemies which seemed to be slain at your feet, will revive, and recover their weapons, and renew the assault in one form or another. And perhaps your most painful combats may be with such as you had thought most easy to be vanquished, and your greatest danger may arise from some of those enemies from whom you had apprehended the least; particularly from pride, and from indolence of spirit; from a secret alienation of heart from God, and from an indisposition for conversing with Him, through an immoderate attachment to things seen and temporal, which may be oftentimes exceeding dangerous to your salvation, though perhaps they be not absolutely and universally prohibited. In a thousand of these instances you must learn to deny yourself, or you cannot be Christ's disciple.

You must also lay your account to find great difficulties from the world; from its manners, customs, and examples. The things of the world will hinder you one way, and the men of the world another. . . . The enemies of religion will be bold and active in their assaults, while many of its friends seem unconcerned; and one sinner will probably exert himself more to corrupt you, than ten Christians to secure and save you. . . . You will be derided and insulted by those whose esteem and affection you naturally desire; and may find much more propriety than you imagine in that expression of the apostle, 'the trial of cruel mockings' (Heb. 11.36) which some fear more than either sword or flames. This persecution of the tongue you must expect to go through, and perhaps may be branded as a lunatic for no other cause than that you begin to exercise your reason to purpose, and will not join with those that are destroying their own souls in their wild career of folly and madness.

In the mean time Satan may be doing his utmost to discourage and distress you. He will, no doubt, raise in your imagination the most tempting idea of the gratifications, the indulgences, and companions you are obliged to forsake; and give you the most discouraging and terrifying view of the difficulties, severities and dangers which are (he will persuade you) inseparable from religion. He will not fail to represent God Himself, the fountain of goodness and happiness, as an hard master, whom it is impossible to please. He will perhaps fill you with the most distressful fears, and with cruel and insolent malice glory over you as his slave, when he knows you are the Lord's freeman. At one time he will study, by his vile suggestions, to interrupt you in your duties, as if they gave him an additional power over you. At another time he will endeavour to weary you of your devotion, by influencing you to prolong it to an immoderate and tedious length, lest his power should be exerted upon you when it ceases.

In short, this practised deceiver has artifices which it would require whole volumes to display, with particular cautions against each. And he will follow you with malicious arts and pursuits to the very end of your pilgrimage; and will leave no method unattempted which may be likely to weaken your hands, and to sadden your heart; that if, through the gracious interposition of God, he cannot prevent your final happiness, he may at least impair your peace and your usefulness as you are passing to it.

This is what the people of God feel; and what you will feel, in some degree or other, if you have your lot and portion among them. But after all, be not discouraged: Christ is the captain of your salvation. When we take a survey of these hosts of enemies, we may lift up our head amidst them all, and say, more and greater is He that is with us, than all those that are against us. Trust in the Lord, and you will be like Mount Zion, which cannot be removed, but abideth for ever.

Amidst all the oppositions of earth and hell, look upward, and look forward, and you will feel your heart animated by the view. Your general is near: He is near to aid you: He is near to reward you. When you feel temptations press the hardest, think of Him who endured even the cross itself for your rescue. View the fortitude of your divine leader, and endeavour to march on in His steps. Hearken to His voice, for He proclaims it aloud, 'Behold I come quickly, and my reward is with me. Be thou faithful unto death, and I will give thee a crown of life.' And oh, how bright will it shine, and how long will its lustre last! When the gems that adorn the crowns of monarchs, and pass (instructive thought) from one royal head to another, through succeeding centuries, are melted down in the last flame, it is a crown of glory which fadeth not away.

JOHN WESLEY (1703-1791)

John Wesley was the fifteenth child of a remarkable pair, the Rev Samuel Wesley, the high church rector of Epworth, Lincolnshire, and his wife Susannah. Their eighteenth child, Charles (1707–1788), became closely associated with John, in the 'Holy Club' and in philanthropic activity at Oxford; in the abortive mission to Georgia (1735–1738); in evangelical conversion through the instrumentality of Moravian Brethren; and in the Evangelical Awakening. Charles was, however, no mere camp-follower of his older brother: he initiated the Holy Club; he was converted three days before John; he was, in the early days of field preaching, an effective open-air evangelist. Not so physically strong as John, however, and blessed with a happy home life, Charles gave up itinerant evangelism and devoted himself to pastoral ministry within the constantly expanding Methodist community, and to writing the 7,270 hymns for which he is renowned. John had early realized a divine call to a monumental service — no less than 'to reform the nation, particularly the church, and to spread Scriptural holiness over the land'. In fact, he declared that 'the world was his parish' — and although he did not again visit America, as George Whitefield did, he sent evangelists there. He travelled the length and breadth of Britain, on horseback, until well into his eighties, preaching to vast crowds, and forming the converts — who were often unwelcome in the Anglican churches — into societies which ultimately and inevitably (despite his reluctance, as an Anglican clergyman, to establish a new denomination) developed into the Methodist Church. His life and ministry were overshadowed, however, by the estrangement from Whitefield through the Calvinist/Arminian controversy. In our selected sermon, Wesley states his views on the subject of Predestination; while Whitefield presents his point of view in letters which follow Wesley's sermon.

ON PREDESTINATION

> Whom He did foreknow, He also did predestinate to be conformed to the image of His Son. . . . whom He did predestinate, them He also called: and whom He called, them He also justified: and whom He justified, them He also glorified (Romans 8.29–30).

'Our beloved brother Paul,' says St Peter, 'according to the wisdom given unto him hath written unto you; as also in all his epistles, speaking in them of these things; in which are some things hard to be understood, which they that are unlearned and unstable wrest, as they do also the other Scriptures, unto their own destruction' (2 Peter 3.15–16). It is not improbable that among those things spoken by St Paul which are hard to be understood, the apostle Peter might place what he speaks on this subject in the eighth and ninth chapters of his epistle to the Romans. And it is certain not only the unlearned, but many of the most learned men in the world, and not the unstable only, but many who seemed to be well established in the truths of the Gospel, have, for several centuries 'wrested' these passages 'to their own destruction'.

'Hard to be understood' we may well allow them to be, when we consider how men of the strongest understanding, improved by all the advantages of education, have continually differed in judgment concerning them. And this very consideration, that there is so wide a difference upon the head between men of the greatest learning, sense, and piety, one might imagine would make all who now speak upon the subject exceedingly wary and self-diffident. But I know not how it is, that just the reverse is observed in every part of the Christian world. No writers on earth appear more positive than those who write on this difficult subject. Nay, the same men who, writing upon any other subject are remarkably modest and humble, on this alone lay aside all self-distrust, 'and speak *ex cathedra* infallible'.

This is peculiarly observable of almost all those who assert the absolute degrees. But surely it is possible to avoid this: whatever we propose, may be proposed with modesty, and with deference to those wise and good men who are of a contrary opinion; and the rather, because so much has been said already, on every part of the question, so many volumes have been written, that it is scarcely possible to say anything which has not been said before. All I would offer at present, not to the lovers of contention, but to men of piety and candour, are a few short hints, which perhaps may cast some light on the text above recited.

The more frequently and carefully I have considered it, the more I have been inclined to think that the apostle is not here (as many have supposed) describing a chain of causes and effects (this does not seem to have entered into his heart), but simply showing *the method in which God works; the order* in which the several branches of salvation constantly follow each other. And this, I apprehend, will be clear to any serious and impartial inquirer, surveying the work of God either forward or backward; either from the beginning to the end, or from the end to the beginning.

And, first, let us look forward on the whole work of God in the salvation of man, considering it from the beginning, the first point, till it terminates in glory. The first point is, the foreknowledge of God. God *foreknew* those in every nation who would believe, from the beginning of the world to the consummation of all things. But, in order to throw light upon this dark question, it should be well observed that when we speak of God's foreknowledge, we do not speak according to the nature of things, but after the manner of men. For, if we speak properly, there is no such thing as foreknowledge or afterknowledge in God. All time, or rather all eternity (for time is only that small fragment of eternity which is allotted to the children of men) being present to Him at once, He does not know one thing before another, or one thing after another; but sees all things in one point of view from everlasting to everlasting. As all time, with everything that exists therein, is present with Him at once, so He sees at once whatever was, is, or will be, to the end of time.

But observe: We must not think they are because He knows them. No: He knows them because they are. Just as I (if one may be allowed to compare the things of men with the deep things of God) now know the sun shines: yet the sun does not shine because I know it, but I know it because it shines. My knowledge supposes the sun to shine, but does not in anywise cause it. In like manner, God knows that man sins, for He knows all things; yet we do not sin because He knows it, but He knows it because we sin; and His knowledge supposes our sin, but does not in anywise cause it. In a word, God, looking on all ages, from the creation to the consummation, as a moment, and seeing at once whatever is in the hearts of all the children of men, knows every one that does or does not believe, in every age or nation.

Yet what He knows, whether faith or unbelief, is in nowise caused by His knowledge. Men are as free in believing or not believing as if He did not know it at all.

Indeed, if man were not free, he could not be accountable either for his thoughts, words, or actions. If he were not free, he would not be capable either of reward or punishment; he would be incapable either of virtue or vice, of being either morally good or bad. If he had no more freedom than the sun, the moon, or the stars, he would be no more accountable than them. On supposition that he had no more freedom than them, the stones of the earth would be as capable of reward, and as liable to punishment, as man: one would be as accountable as the other. Yea, and it would be as absurd to ascribe either virtue or vice to him as to ascribe it to the stock of a tree.

But to proceed: 'Whom He did foreknow, them He did predestinate to be conformed to the image of His Son.' This is the second step (to speak after the manner of men: for in fact there is nothing *before* or *after* in God). In other words, God decrees, from everlasting to everlasting, that all who believe in the Son of His love, shall be conformed to His image; shall be saved from all inward and outward sin, into all inward and outward holiness. Accordingly, it is a plain undeniable fact that all who truly believe in the name of the Son of God do now 'receive the end of their faith, the salvation of their souls', and this in virtue of the unchangeable, irreversible, irresistible decree of God. 'He that believeth shall be saved'; 'he that believeth not shall be damned.'

'Whom He did predestinate, them He also called.' This is the third step (still remembering that we speak after the manner of men). To express it a little more largely: according to His fixed decree that believers shall be saved, those whom He foreknows as such, He calls both outwardly and inwardly — *outwardly* by the word of His grace, and *inwardly* by His Spirit. This inward application of His word to the heart seems to be what some term 'effectual calling'. And it implies the calling them children of God; the accepting them 'in the Beloved'; the justifying them 'freely by His grace, through the redemption that is in Jesus Christ'.

'Whom He called, them He justified.' This is the fourth step. It is generally allowed that the word 'justified' here is taken in a peculiar sense: that it means He made them just or righteous. He executed His decree, 'conforming them to the image of His Son', or, as we usually speak, sanctified them.

It remains, 'whom He justified, them He also glorified'. This is the last step. Having made them 'meet to be partakers of the inheritance of the saints in light', He gives them 'the kingdom which was prepared for them before the world began'. This is the order wherein, 'according to the counsel of His will', the plan He has laid down from eternity, He saves those whom He foreknew — the true believers in every place and generation.

The same great work of salvation by faith, according to the foreknowledge and decree of God, may appear in a still clearer light if we view it backward, from the end to the beginning. Suppose then you stood with the 'great multitude which no man can number, out of every nation, and tongue, and kindred and people', who 'give praise unto Him that sitteth upon the throne, and unto the Lamb for ever and ever', you would not find one among them all that were entered into glory, who was not a witness of that great truth, 'Without holiness no man shall see the Lord'; not one of all that innumerable company who was not sanctified before he was glorified. By holiness he was prepared for glory according to the invariable will of the Lord that the crown, purchased by the blood of His Son, should be given to none but those who are renewed by His Spirit. He is become 'the author of eternal salvation' only 'to them that obey Him'; that obey Him inwardly and outwardly; that are holy in heart, and holy in all manner of conversation.

And could you take a view of all those upon earth who are now sanctified, you would find not one of these had been sanctified until after he was called. He was first called, not only with an outward call, by the word and the messengers of God, but likewise with an inward call, by His Spirit applying His word, enabling him to believe in the only-begotten Son of God, and bearing testimony with his spirit that he was a child of God. And it was by this very means they were all sanctified. It was by a sense of the love of God shed abroad in his heart, that every one of them was enabled to love God. Loving God, he loved his neighbour as himself, and had power to walk in all His commandments blameless. This is a rule which admits of no exception. God calls a sinner His own, that is, justifies him, before He sanctifies. And by this very thing, the consciousness of His favour, He works in him that grateful, filial affection, from which springs every good temper, and word, and work.

And who are they who are thus called of God, but those whom He had before predestinated, or decreed, to 'conform to the image of His Son'? This decree (still speaking after the manner of men) precedes every man's calling: every believer was predestinated before he was called. For God calls none but 'according to the counsel of His will', according to this plan of acting which He laid down before the foundation of the world.

Once more, as all that are called were predestinated, so all whom God has predestinated He foreknew. He knew, He saw them as believers, and as such predestinated them to salvation according to His eternal decree, 'He that believeth shall be saved'. Thus we see the whole process of the work of God, from the end to the beginning. Who are glorified? None but those who were first justified. Who are justified? None but those who were first predestinated. Who are predestinated? None but those whom God foreknew as believers. Thus the purpose and word of God stand unshaken as the pillars of heaven: 'He that believeth shall be saved; he that believeth not shall be damned.' And thus God is clear from the blood of all men; since whoever perishes, perishes by his own act and deed. 'They will not come unto me,' says the Saviour of men; and 'there is no salvation in any other'. They 'will not believe', and there is no other way either to present or eternal salvation. Therefore their blood is upon their own head; and God is still 'justified in His saying' that He 'willeth all men to be saved, and to come to the knowledge of the truth'.

The sum of all is this: the almighty, all-wise God sees and knows, from everlasting to everlasting, all that is, that was, and that is to come, through one eternal *now*. With Him nothing is either past or future, but all things equally present. He has, therefore, if we speak according to the truth of all things, no foreknowledge, no after-knowledge. This would be ill consistent with the apostle's words, 'With Him is no variableness or shadow of turning', and with the account he gives of Himself by the prophet, 'I the Lord change not'. Yet when He speaks to us, knowing whereof we are made, knowing the scantiness of our understanding, He lets Himself down to our capacity, and speaks of Himself after the manner of men. Thus, in condescention to our weakness, He speaks of His own purpose, counsel, plan, foreknowledge. Not that God has any need of counsel, of purpose, or of planning His work beforehand. Far be it from us to impute these to the Most High, to measure Him by ourselves! It is merely in compassion to us that He speaks thus of Himself, as foreknowing the things in heaven or earth, and as predestinating or fore-ordaining them. But can we possibly imagine that these expressions are to be taken literally? To one who was so gross in his conceptions might He not say, 'Thinkest thou I am such an one as thyself?' Not so: as the heavens are higher than the earth, so are my ways higher than thy ways. I know, decree, work in such a manner as it is not possible for thee to conceive: but to give thee some faint, glimmering knowledge of my ways, I use the language of men, and suit myself to thy apprehension in this thy infant state of existence.

What is it, then, that we learn from this whole account? It is this, and no more: (1) God knows all believers; (2) wills that they should be saved from sin; (3) to that end, justifies them, (4) sanctifies them, and (5) takes them to glory.

O that men would praise the Lord for this His goodness; and that they would be content with this plain account of it, and not endeavour to wade into those mysteries which are too deep for angels to fathom!

GEORGE WHITEFIELD (1714-1770)

The son of an inn-keeper in Gloucester, George Whitefield was educated in that city and at Oxford University, where he became a member of the 'Holy Club' in which Charles and John Wesley were the leading spirits—in that order, since it was Charles who initiated the group of 'the first Methodists' of which John later became the dominant personality. After ordination, Whitefield preached his first sermon in Gloucester, with such fervour that complaint was made to the Bishop that he had driven 15 people mad! Shortly afterwards he went to America, at the invitation of John Wesley; but when he arrived in Georgia Wesley had left for home, disheartened and disillusioned concerning his own spiritual state. Whitefield established promising contacts there, and on his return to England raised funds for an orphanage which he established at Savannah during subsequent visits to America. Finding church doors closed to him, he began preaching in the open air—a practice adopted by John and Charles Wesley, and followed henceforth by all three, with dramatic results. Doctrinal differences unhappily parted Whitefield from the Wesleys (see Introduction). Among the most interesting and rewarding writings of George Whitefield are his letters, of which the following four are illuminating examples.

To Mr H., of Gloucester

Oxon, Oct 14, 1736.

Dearest Sir,

I was agreeably detained, as you was pleased to term it, last Tuesday, in reading your kind letter, and had I not been assisted by the grace of God to receive every thing with an equal, undisturbed mind, perhaps the contents of it might have given me some small uneasiness. But religion quite changes the nature of man, and makes us to receive all the dispensations of providence with resignation and thankfulness. Of this, dearest Sir, I hope you have had an experimental proof, in bearing up with courage and resolution under those acute pains the Almighty was pleased to visit you with last Sunday, and with which, perhaps, His infinite wisdom and goodness may continue to visit you longer. My dear friend (if I mistake not) used to say he was afraid God did not love him, because He did not chasten him. Behold then, now the hand of the Lord is upon you, not so much to punish, as to purify your soul. Not in anger but in love. Pray therefore in your easy intervals, that you may know wherefore the Lord contendeth with you, and that you may not come cankered out of the furnace of affliction. Offer up every groan, every sigh, in the name of your dying, risen Redeemer, and doubt not but they will be as prevalent as set times of prayer. Our being enabled to pray when sickness comes on us, doubtless, is to teach us the necessity of praying always, when we are in health. But, dear Mr H. wants no such lessons, or excitements, I believe, to prayer.

Methinks I could bear some of your pain for you, if that would give you comfort. But as it is impossible, O let me never cease most earnestly to beseech my heavenly Father that He would sanctify this His fatherly correction to you, and that the sense of your weakness may add strength to your faith, and seriousness to your repentance.

Poor Mr Pauncefoot, I find, is visited in a far more grievous manner. Dear good man, surely the time of his dissolution (I should say of his coronation) draweth near. See, dear Mr H. through what tribulations we must enter into glory. Be pleased to give my hearty love and thanks to him for his last kind letter. Beg him not to cease praying for me, unworthy as I am. And, I hope, I shall not be wanting in returning his kindness in the same manner. But alas, I have nothing to depend on, but the merits of a crucified Redeemer to have my poor petitions answered.

But does dear Mrs H. complain of deadness and coldness in devotion? Alas poor woman! let her not be disheartened. This is a complaint which all the children of God have made. And we must take a great deal of pains with our hearts, must pray often and long, before we shall be able to pray well. And the only way I can think of, to shame ourselves out of deadness in prayer, is to censure and condemn, to humble and bewail ourselves for it every time we go upon our knees, at least every time we solemnly retire to converse with God.

But why does Mrs H. so much as think of omitting but once the receiving of the holy sacrament? Or if Satan does put such thoughts in her head, why does she not repel them with the utmost abhorrence? Alas! should the devil gain his point here, would not the ridiculing world say, Mrs H. began to build, but had not wherewith to finish. I have seen too many fatal instances of the inexpressible danger and sad consequences of leaving off any one means of grace, not to encourage Mrs H. stedfastly to persevere in the good way she has begun; and would exhort her, in the name of the Lord Jesus Christ, to labour daily to mortify and subdue her corruptions, not wilfully indulge herself in any habit, custom, or temper, and then assure herself, one time or another, Christ will be made known to her in breaking of bread . . .

To the Reverend Mr John Wesley

Charles-Town, Aug 25, 1740.

Dear and Honoured Sir,

Last night I had the pleasure of receiving an extract of your journal. This morning I took a walk and read it. I pray God to give it His blessing. Many things I trust will prove beneficial, especially the account of yourself. Only, give me leave with all humility to exhort you not to be strenuous in opposing the doctrines of election and final perseverance, when, by your own confession, 'you have not the witness of the Spirit within yourself', and consequently are not a proper judge. I remember dear brother E--- told me one day that 'he was convinced of the perseverance of the saints'. I told him you was not. He replied, but he will be convinced when he hath got the Spirit himself. I am assured, God has now for some years given me this living witness in my soul. I cannot say I have since indulged any doubts (at least for no considerable time) about the forgiveness of my sins; nay, I can scarce say that I ever doubted at all. When I have been nearest death, my evidences have been the clearest. I can say I have been on the borders of Canaan, and do every day, nay, almost every moment, long for the appearing of our Lord Jesus Christ; not to evade sufferings, but with a single desire to see His blessed face. I feel His blessed Spirit daily filling my soul and body, as plain as I feel the air which I breathe, or the food I eat.

Perhaps the doctrines of election and of final perseverance hath been abused (and what doctrine has not), but notwithstanding, it is children's bread, and ought not in my opinion to be withheld from them, supposing it is always mentioned with proper cautions against the abuse. Dear and Honoured Sir, I write not this to enter into disputation. I hope, at this time, I feel something of the meekness and gentleness of Christ. I cannot bear the thoughts of opposing you: but how can I avoid it if you go about (as your brother C-- once said) to drive John Calvin out of Bristol. Alas, I never read any thing that Calvin wrote; my doctrine I had from Christ and His apostles; I was taught them of God; and as God was pleased to send me out first, and to enlighten me first, so I think He still continues to do it. My business seems to be chiefly in planting; if God send you to water, I praise His name. I wish you a thousandfold increase.

I find, by young W--'s letter, there is disputing among you about election, and perfection. I pray God to put a stop to it, for what good end will it answer? I wish I knew your principles fully; did you write oftner (*sic*), and more frankly, it might have a better effect than silence and reserve. I have lately had many domestic trials, and that about points of doctrine, not by myself, but from others in my absence. I daily wait upon God, depending on His promise that all things, even this, shall work together for my good. Many in Charles Town, I believe, are called of God. You may now find a Christian without searching the town as with a candle. Mr G--- is less furious, at least in public. He hath expended all his strength, and finds he cannot prevail.

Adieu, Honoured Sir, Adieu! My health is better, since I last left Charles Town, and am now freed from domestic cares. With almost tears of love to you, and the brethren, do I subscribe myself, honoured Sir,

Your most affectionate brother and servant in Christ,

G. W.

To Mr A---

Boston, Sept 23, 1740.

My dear Brother A---

I thank you for your letter: may the Lord enable me to send you an answer of peace. Sinless perfection, I think, is unattainable in this life. Shew me a man that could ever justly say, 'I am perfect'. It is enough if we can say so when we bow down our heads and give up the ghost. Indwelling sin remains till death, even in the regenerate, as the article of the church expresses it. There is no man that liveth and sinneth not in thought, word, and deed. However, to affirm such a thing as perfection and to deny final perseverance, what an absurdity is this? To be incapable of sinning, and capable of being finally damned, is a contradiction in terms. From such doctrine may I ever turn away!

Labour, dear Mr A---, to be holy, even as God is holy; but do not look for complete perfection here below. What is this, but in effect to vacate the righteousness of Christ? I hear many amongst you who begun (*sic*) in the Spirit, are now ending in the flesh. Christ hath freely justified them, *i.e.* entitled them to all His merits, and yet they must do so and so to keep themselves in a justified state. Alas, this is sorry divinity; I have not so learned Christ. No, His gifts and callings are without repentance. Whom He loves, He loves to the end. Work I will, but not to keep myself in a justified state. My Lord hath secured that; but I will work to shew my gratitude for His putting me into a justified state. O that all would study the covenant of grace.

Dear Mr A--- I feel that I love you, and I find myself carried out to write in this manner. My Lord blesses me with all spiritual blessings; He causes me to rejoice in His salvation. I pray Him to carry on His work in London, and to keep His church from errors; but there must be a sifting as well as a gathering time. It is meet that such offences should come. All shall work together for good to those who are *called after God's purpose*: they shall finally be saved. This much comforts, dear Brother A---,

Your affectionate brother in Christ,

G. W.

To Mr F---, in Pensylvania.

Edinburgh, Sept 22, 1742.

My dear Brother F---,

I received your two kind letters, dated June 1st and 6th, and can only say, Christ is King in Zion, and orders all things well. I think you cannot have a scene of greater confusion among you, than there has been in England. But blessed be God, matters are brought to a better issue, and though we cannot agree in principles, yet we agree in love. Tho', as you know, I am clear in the truths of the Gospel, yet I find that principles of themselves, without the Spirit of God, will not unite any set of men whatever; and where the Spirit of God is in any great degree, there will be union of heart, though there may be difference in sentiments. This I have learnt, my dear brother, by happy experience, and find great freedom and peace in my soul thereby. This makes me to love many, though I cannot agree with them in some of their principles. I dare not look on them as wilful deceivers, but as persons who hazard their lives for the sake of the Gospel.

Mr W(esley) I think is wrong in some things, and Mr L--- wrong also; yet I believe that both Mr L--- and Mr W---, and others with whom we do not agree in all things, will shine bright in glory. It is best therefore for a Gospel-minister simply and powerfully to preach those truths he has been taught of God, and to meddle as little as possible with those who are children of God, though they should differ in many things. This would keep the heart sweet, and at the same time not betray the truths of Jesus. I have tried both the disputing and the quiet way, and find the latter far preferable to the former. I have not given way to the Moravian Brethren, or Mr W---y, or to any whom I thought in error, no not for an hour. But I think it best not to dispute when there is no probability of convincing. I pray you, for Christ's sake, to take heed lest your spirit should be imbittered (*sic*) when you are speaking or writing for God. This will give your adversaries advantage over you, and make people think your passion is the effect of your principles. Since I have been in England this time, Calvin's example has been much pressed upon me. You know how Luther abused him. As we are of Calvinistical principles, I trust we shall in this respect imitate Calvin's practice, and shew all meekness to those who may oppose.

My dear brother, you will not be offended at my using this freedom. I am a poor creature, unworthy to advise you; but I simply tell you a little of my own experience. May the Lord give you, and all that stand up for the doctrines of the Gospel, a right judgment in all things! For Jesus Christ's sake, as much as in you lies, put a stop to disputing. It imbitters (*sic*) the spirit, ruffles the soul, and hinders it from hearing the small still voice of the Holy Ghost. May you be filled with all joy and peace in believing! God has been very gracious to me here. Wonderful things have been done in Scotland. When I shall come to you, I cannot as yet determine. I hope to embark in a few months. In the mean time, be pleased to remember me to all that love the glorious Emmanuel, and accept this in tenderest love from, my very dear brother,

Your most affectionate though most unworthy brother and servant in the kingdom and patience of Jesus.

G. W.

HENRY VENN (1724-1797)

The descendant of a long line of clergymen, Henry Venn was born at Barnes, in Surrey, and educated at Cambridge. After several curacies he became vicar of Huddersfield, Yorkshire, in 1759, and found the town 'dark, ignorant, immoral'. Through his ministry it was, however, 'shaken in the centre by the lever of the Gospel'. Health reasons led him to move to the vicarage of Yelling, in Huntingdonshire, in 1771, where his preaching attracted the attention of the Countess of Huntingdon, William Cowper, and a younger man destined to exercise a profound influence in the church, Charles Simeon. Henry Venn spent the last six months of his life at Clapham, where his son John was rector, and leader of the 'Clapham Sect' of wealthy philanthropists, including William Wilberforce, who were closely associated with the founding of the Church Missionary Society and the British and Foreign Bible Society. Of Henry Venn's two books, *The Complete Duty of Man* is widely regarded as a religious classic. From it our selection is taken from the chapter on 'The Dispositions of a Christian Towards God'.

THE DISPOSITIONS OF A CHRISTIAN TOWARDS GOD

As God is altogether lovely in Himself, and in His benefits towards us inexpressibly great, so nothing can be more evident than that He ought to reign in our affections without a rival. But to yield this most rightful worship to his Creator, man is naturally averse: and it is owing to the peculiar doctrines of the Gospel, enforced by the power of the Holy Spirit, that the Christian renounces his natural disaffection to his Creator, and glorifies Him as God . . .

We begin with those various dispositions towards the ever-blessed God, of which the habitual exercise is to be found in the heart of every real Christian.

The first disposition of this kind is *fear*. This is one of those great springs of action by which rational creatures are influenced. It is of the highest importance therefore to have this affection exercised upon some just object, so that the mind may, on the one hand, be armed against vain terrors, and, on the other, be duly impressed by those things which ought to be dreaded. In this excellent manner the affection of fear is regulated in the Christian's breast. Temporal evils of every kind he discerns to be nothing more than instruments in the hand of God, wholly subserving His pleasure, and unable to affect man's most important interest. Therefore he 'sanctifies the Lord God in his heart', and regards as 'his fear and his dread' Him who is too wise to be deceived, too just to be biased, too mighty to be resisted, and too majestic to be contemplated without reverence and self-abasement. Very different is his fear of the Most High from the terror of a slave, that uneasy feeling which causes the object of it to be considered with pain. His is the fear of a rational creature towards its all-perfect Creator, of a servant towards a tender master, of a child towards its wise and merciful father. Therefore, in the same proportion as he increases in the knowledge of God, he increases also in the fear of Him . . .

A Christian fears the Lord, so as to stand in awe: he can neither be bribed, nor intimidated, wilfully to sin against Him. . . . But as he is encompassed with infirmities, snares, and temptations, so he finds it necessary at some seasons, to the end of his life, to repel solicitations to evil by reflecting upon the severity of God's vengeance on impenitent sinners; and by meditating upon the wrath of God revealed from heaven against all ungodliness and unrighteousness of men. In this fear of the Lord is safety; and the longer he lives under its influence, the more it becomes a generous filial fear.

This fear therefore does not hinder, but promotes the exercise of another disposition towards God, which is most conspicuous in every real Christian, namely, *a readiness to obey God without reserve*. He beholds his Maker's absolute dominion over him founded in his very being. Every faculty of his soul, and every member of his body, is a witness of his Maker's righteous claim to his life and to his labours; when He requires them to be employed in His service, He does but appoint the use of what is His own absolute property. Ever conscious of this, he resolutely regards the authority of God in a world which despises it; he uniformly persists in obedience to Him, though his natural corruptions, his worldly interest, and the prevailing customs of the world should oppose it. In his judgment, the command of God alone constitutes a practice reasonable and necessary. He wants no higher authority to confirm it; nor can any objections from selfish considerations induce him to evade its force, or prevaricate with respect to the obligation of the command. He makes his prayer unto the God of his life, to teach him His statutes; to set his heart at liberty from every evil bias, that he may run the way of His commandments. . . .

Gratitude to God is also a distinguishing part of the Christian disposition. Where there is any degree of honesty and generosity of mind, there will necessarily be a desire also of testifying a due sense of favours received; an eagerness to embrace the first opportunity of convincing our Friend and Benefactor that we feel our obligations. In the case of benefits and favours conferred by man upon man, all acknowledge the duty of this grateful return, and are ready to brand with ignominy the ingrate who repays with ill-will or neglect his liberal patron. But, alas! where the obligation is the greatest possible it is often the least felt, and men scruple not to treat with neglect the supreme Benefactor of the human race. From this detestable crime the real Christian alone stands exempted. He perceives cogent and continual reasons for gratitude to God, and is impressed by them.

But much more is he excited to thankfulness upon considering the mercies relating to his eternal interest. He freely acknowledges that God might have justly cut him off whilst he was living in rebellion against His law; or have left him to continue under that dreadful hardness and blindness of heart which so long had power over him. Instead of this, he can say, 'He hath opened my eyes and changed my heart; conquered the stubbornness of my will, and given me an un-feigned desire to be conformed to His; made me a member of Christ; persuaded me by His Spirit of the truth and absolute necessity of redemption by the Son of God. I am able, in some degree, to comprehend with all saints the length and breadth, the height and depth of the love of Christ. I have a distinct view of the long train of reproaches, miseries, and torments, which my salvation cost the Lord of life and glory. I behold, on the one hand, the fathomless abyss of woe from which He has rescued me; on the other, the eternal glory He has promised for my inheritance. Whilst I meditate on all these things, and grow more and more intimately acquainted with their truth, I feel upon my mind an increasing conviction that the Lord hath dealt bountifully with me. I am glad to confess that no slave can be so absolutely the property of his master, as I am of God; nor any pensioner, though supported by the most rich and undeserved bounty, so strongly engaged to gratitude, as I am to glorify God both with my body and with my soul, which are His.'

That such is the prevailing sentiment of a Christian, is evident from the apostle's declaration. When he is shewing the powerful motive which influenced him, and all the followers of the Lamb, to such eminent zeal in His service, he says, 'The love of Christ con-straineth us'; with a pleasing force it bears down all opposition before it, like a mighty torrent, and carries forth our souls in all the actings of an ingenuous gratitude and thankfulness towards God.

JOHN NEWTON (1725-1807)

Following a turbulent childhood, John Newton was 'press ganged' into the Royal Navy, and on escaping became, in West Africa, virtually the slave of a white slave-trader's black wife. Becoming involved in the slave trade, he was dramatically converted in 1747 during a violent storm at sea. He still engaged in the slave traffic, however, until convicted of its wrong in 1755; and after ordination in 1764 he became curate at Olney, Buckinghamshire, where he befriended the unhappy William Cowper and collaborated with him in producing the renowned 'Olney hymns', including 'Amazing Grace'. In 1779 Newton was appointed vicar of St Mary Woolnoth in the City of London, and there became one of the outstanding preachers of the metropolis. In later years he collaborated with William Wilberforce in the campaign for abolishing the slave trade. Many correspondents sought his help, and his letters are regarded as his finest literary achievement. He has been described as 'the letter writer *par excellence* of the Evangelical Revival: this was his distinctive contribution to that great movement'. In 'Letter 13' he gave wise and practical counsel on the theme of divine guidance.

DIVINE GUIDANCE

It is well for those who are duly sensible of their own weakness and fallibility, and of the difficulties with which they are surrounded in life, that the Lord has promised to guide His people with His eye, and to cause them to hear a word behind them, saying 'This is the way, walk ye in it', when they are in danger of turning aside either to the right hand or to the left. For this purpose, He has given us the written Word to be a lamp to our feet, and encouraged us to pray for the teaching of His Holy Spirit, that we may rightly understand and apply it. It is, however, too often seen that many widely deviate from the path of duty, and commit gross and perplexing mistakes, while they profess a sincere desire to know the will of God, and think they have His warrant and authority. This must certainly be owing to misapplication of the rule by which they judge, since the rule itself is infallible, and the promises sure. The Scripture cannot deceive us, if rightly understood; but it may, if perverted, prove the occasion of confirming us in a mistake. The Holy Spirit cannot mislead those who are under His influence; but we may suppose that we are so when we are not. It may not be unseasonable to offer a few thoughts upon a subject of great importance to the peace of our minds, and to the honour of our holy profession.

Many have been deceived as to what they ought to do, or in forming a judgment beforehand of events in which they are nearly concerned, by expecting direction in ways which the Lord has not warranted. I shall mention some of the principal of these, for it is not easy to enumerate them all.

Some persons, when two or more things have been in view, and they could not immediately determine which to prefer, have committed their case to the Lord by prayer, and have then proceeded to cast lots, taking it for granted that after such a solemn appeal the turning up of the lot might be safely rested in as an answer from God. It is true, that the Scripture, and indeed right reason, assures us that the Lord disposes the lot; and there are several cases recorded in the Old Testament in which lots were used by divine appointment; but I think neither these, nor the choosing Matthias by lot to the apostleship, are proper precedents for our conduct.

In the division of the lands of Canaan, in the affair of Achan, and in the nomination of Saul to the kingdom, recourse was had to the lot by God's express command. The instance of Matthias likewise was singular, such as can never happen again; namely, the choice of an apostle who would not have been upon a par with the rest, who were chosen immediately by the Lord, unless *He* had been pleased to interpose in some extraordinary way; and all these were before the canon of Scripture was completed, and before the full descent and communication of the Holy Spirit, who was promised to dwell with the church to the end of time. Under the New Testament dispensa- tion we are invited to come boldly to the throne of grace, to make our requests known to the Lord, and to cast our cares upon Him: but we have neither precept nor promise respecting the use of lots; and to have recourse to them without His appointment seems to be tempting Him rather than honouring Him, and to savour more of presumption than dependence. The effects likewise of this expedient have often been unhappy and hurtful: a sufficient proof how little it is to be trusted to as a guide of our conduct.

Others, when in doubt, have opened the Bible at a venture, and expected to find something to direct them in the first verse they should cast their eye upon. It is no small discredit to this practice that the heathens, who knew not the Bible, used some of their favourite books in the same way; and grounded their persuasions of what they ought to do, or of what should befall them, according to the passage they happened to open upon. Among the Romans the writings of Virgil were frequently consulted upon these occasions, which gave rise to the well-known expression of the *Sortes Virgilianae*. And, indeed, Virgil is as well adapted to satisfy inquirers in this way, as the Bible itself; for if people will be governed by the occurrence of a single text of Scripture, without regarding the context or duly comparing it with the general tenor of the Word of God, and with their own circumstances, they may commit the greatest ex- travagances, expect the greatest impossibilities, and contradict the plainest dictates of common sense, while they think they have the Word of God on their side. Can the opening upon 2 Samuel 7.3, when Nathan said to David, 'Do all that is in thine heart, for the Lord is with thee', be sufficient to determine the lawfulness or ex- pediency of actions? Or can a glance of the eye upon our Lord's words to the woman of Canaan, Matthew 15.28, 'Be it unto thee even as thou wilt', amount to a proof that the present earnest desire of the mind (whatever it may be) shall be surely accomplished? Yet it is certain that matters big with important consequences have been engaged in, and the most sanguine expectations formed, upon no better warrant than dipping (as it is called) upon a text of Scripture.

A sudden strong impression of a text that seems to have some resemblance to the concern upon the mind, has been accepted by many as an infallible token that they were right, and that things would go just as they would have them; or, on the other hand, if the passage bore a threatening aspect, it has filled them with fears and disquietudes, which they have afterwards found were groundless and unnecessary. These impressions, being more out of their power than the former method, have been more generally regarded and trusted to, but have frequently proved no less delusive. It is allowed that such impressions of a precept or a promise as humble, animate, or comfort the soul, by giving it a lively sense of the truth contained in the words, are both profitable and pleasant; and many of the Lord's people have been instructed and supported (especially in a time of trouble) by some seasonable word of grace applied and sealed by the Spirit with power to their hearts. But if impressions or impulses are received as a voice from heaven, directing to such particular actions as could not be proved to be duties without them, a person may be unwarily misled into great evils and gross delusions; and many have been so. There is no doubt but that the enemy of our souls, if permitted, can furnish us with Scriptures in abundance in this way, and for these purposes.

Some persons judge of the nature and event of their designs by the freedom which they find in prayer. They say they commit their ways to God, seek His direction, and are favoured with much enlargement of spirit; and therefore they cannot doubt but what they have in view is acceptable in the Lord's sight. I would not absolutely reject every plea of this kind, yet without other corroborating evidence.I could not admit it in proof of what it is brought for. It is not *always* easy to determine when we have spiritual freedom in prayer. Self is deceitful; and when our hearts are much fixed and bent upon a thing, this may put words and earnestness into our mouths. Too often we first secretly determine for ourselves, and then come to ask counsel of God; in such a disposition we are ready to catch at everything that may seem to favour our darling scheme; and the Lord, for the detection and chastisement of our hypocrisy (for hypocrisy it is, though perhaps hardly perceptible to ourselves), may answer us according to our idols: see Ezekiel 14.3–4. Besides, the grace of prayer may be in exercise when the subject-matter of the prayer may be founded upon a mistake, from the intervention of circumstances which we are unacquainted with. Thus I may have a friend in a distant country; I hope he is alive, I pray for him, and it is my duty to do so. The Lord by His Spirit assists His people in what is their present duty. If I am enabled to pray with much liberty for my distant friend it may be a proof that the Spirit of the Lord is pleased to assist my infirmities, but it is no proof that my friend is certainly alive at the time I am praying for him; and if the next time I pray for him I should find my spirit straitened, I am not to conclude that my friend is dead, and therefore the Lord will not assist me in praying for him any longer.

Once more: A remarkable dream has sometimes been thought as decisive as any of the foregoing methods of knowing the will of God. That many wholesome and seasonable admonitions have been received in dreams, I willingly allow; but though they may be occasionally noticed, to pay a great attention to dreams, especially to be guided by them to form our sentiments, conduct, or expectations upon them, is superstitious and dangerous. The promises are not made to those who dream, but to those who watch.

Upon the whole, though the Lord may give some persons, upon some occasions, a hint or encouragement out of the common way; yet expressly to look for and seek His direction in such things as I have mentioned, is unscriptural and ensnaring. I could fill many sheets with a detail of the inconveniences and evils which have followed such a dependence, within the course of my own observation. I have seen some presuming they were doing God service, while acting in contradiction to His express commands. I have known others infatuated to believe a lie, declaring themselves assured beyond the shadow of a doubt of things which, after all, never came to pass; and when at length disappointed, Satan has improved the occasion to make them doubt of the plainest and most important truths, and to account their whole former experience a delusion. By these things weak believers have been stumbled, cavils and offences against the Gospel multiplied, and the ways of truth evil spoken of.

But how then may the Lord's guidance be expected? After what has been premised negatively, the question may be answered in a few words. In general, He guides and directs His people by affording them, in answer to prayer, the light of His Holy Spirit, which enables them to understand and to love the Scriptures. The Word of God is not to be used as a lottery; nor is it designed to instruct us by shreds and scraps, which, detached from their proper places, have no determinate import; but it is to furnish us with just principles, right apprehensions to regulate our judgments and affections, and thereby to influence and direct our conduct. They who study the Scriptures in an humble dependence upon divine teaching, are convinced of their own weakness, are taught to make a true estimate of everything around them, are gradually formed into a spirit of submission to the will of God, discover the nature and duties of their several situations and relations in life, and the snares and temptations to which they are exposed. The Word of God dwells richly in them, is a preservative from error, a light to their feet, and a spring of strength and consolation. By treasuring up the doctrines, precepts, promises, examples, and exhortations of Scripture in their minds, and daily comparing themselves with the rule by which they walk, they grow into an habitual frame of spiritual wisdom, and acquire a gracious taste which enables them to judge of right and wrong with a degree of readiness and certainty, as a musical ear judges of sounds. And they are seldom mistaken, because they are influenced by the love of Christ which rules in their hearts, and a regard to the glory of God, which is the great object they have in view.

In particular cases the Lord opens and shuts for them, breaks down walls of difficulty which obstruct their path, or hedges up their way with thorns when they are in danger of going wrong, by the dispensations of His providence. They know that their concernments are in His hands; they are willing to follow whither and when He leads; but are afraid of going before Him. Therefore they are not impatient: because they believe, they will not make haste, but wait daily upon Him in prayer; especially when they find their hearts most engaged in any purpose or pursuit, they are most jealous of being deceived by appearances, and dare not move farther or faster than they can perceive His light shining upon their paths. I express at least their desire, if not their attainment: thus they would be. And though there are seasons when faith languishes, and self too much prevails, this is their general disposition; and the Lord whom they serve does not disappoint their expectations. He leads them by a right way, preserves them from a thousand snares, and satisfies them that He is and will be their guide even unto death.

JOHN WILLIAM FLETCHER (OF MADELEY)
(1729-1785)

Almost invariably known as 'Fletcher of Madeley', John William Fletcher has also the distinction of being renowned for saintliness of character and life. Born and educated in Switzerland (his original name was Jean Guillaume de la Fléchère), he came to England in 1752, was converted under the influence of the Methodists, and ordained by the Bishop of Bangor in 1757. He assisted Wesley in London, and became one of his closest friends. In 1760 he was appointed vicar of Madeley, in Shropshire, and in addition to devoted pastoral ministry and assistance to Wesley engaged voluminously—but graciously—in the Calvinist-Arminian controversy which characterized the time. Described as 'an Arminian of the Arminians', he issued five 'Blasts Against Antinomianism'—as he described Calvinism. But he always wrote in Christian restraint and love, winning the esteem and affection even of his opponents. After his death the manuscripts of six 'Spiritual Letters' were found, apparently written in the earlier part of his life, but it is not known to whom they were addressed. The sixth of these discusses 'Spiritual Manifestations of the Son of God'.

SPIRITUAL MANIFESTATIONS OF THE SON OF GOD

The New Testament abounds, as well as the Old, with accounts of particular revelations of the Son of God. Before His birth He manifested Himself to the Blessed Virgin by the overshadowing power of the Holy Ghost. She *rejoiced in God her Saviour*, and glorified more in having Him revealed as God in her soul, than in finding Him conceived as man in her womb. Soon after, Joseph her husband was assured in a heavenly dream that the child she bore was *Emmanuel, God with us*. He revealed Himself next to Elizabeth. When she *heard the salutation of Mary, she was filled with the Holy Ghost*, and made sensible that the virgin was the mother of her Lord. So powerful was this manifestation that her unborn son was affected by it. *The babe leaped in her womb for joy*, and *was filled with the Holy Ghost even from his mother's womb*.

So important is a particular knowledge of Jesus that an angel directed the shepherds, and a miraculous star the wise men, to the place where He was born; and there the Holy Ghost so revealed Him to their hearts that they hesitated not to worship the seemingly despicable infant, as the majestic God whom the heaven of heavens cannot contain.

Simeon, who 'waited for the consolation of Israel', had it 'revealed to him by the Holy Ghost that he should not see death before he had seen the Lord's Christ'. The promise was fulfilled; and while his bodily eyes discovered nothing but a poor infant, presented without pomp in the temple, his spiritual eyes perceived Him to be the light of Israel, and the salvation of God. Nor was this extraordinary favour granted only to Simeon, for it is written, 'All flesh shall see the salvation of God'; and St Luke informs us that Anna partook of the sight with the old Israelite, gave thanks to her new born Lord, and 'spake of Him to all that waited for redemption in Jerusalem'.

When He entered upon His ministry, He first manifested Himself to His forerunner. 'I knew Him not' personally, said John: 'but He that sent me to baptize with water said unto me, upon whom thou shalt see the Spirit descending, and remaining on Him, the same is He who baptizes with the Holy Ghost. And I saw, and bear record that this is the Son of God, the Lamb that taketh away the sins of the world.'

Jesus had manifested Himself spiritually to Nathanael under the fig tree; and the honest Israelite, being reminded of that divine favour, confessed the author of it: 'Rabbi,' said he, 'Thou art the Son of God; Thou art the King of Israel.' Our Lord, pleased with this ready confession, promised that he should see greater things, enjoy brighter manifestations than these; that he should even 'see heaven open, and the angels of God ascending and descending upon the Son of man'.

The bare outward sight of our Saviour's person and miracles rather confounded than converted the beholders. What glorious beams of His Godhead pierced through the veil of His mean appearances when, with supreme authority, He turned the buyers and sellers out of the temple; when He entered Jerusalem in triumph, and all the city was moved, saying, 'Who is this?'; and when He said to those who apprehended Him, 'I am He', and they went backward and fell on the ground! Nevertheless, we do not find that one person was blessed with the saving knowledge of Him on any of these solemn occasions. The people of Galilee saw most of Him, and yet believed least in Him. 'What wisdom is this, which is given to this man,' said they, 'that such mighty works are wrought by His hands? Is not this the carpenter, the son of Mary?' And they were offended at Him. Some went even so far as to ascribe His miracles to a diabolical power, affirming that He cast out devils by Beelzebub the prince of the devils. Hence it appears that if He had not in some degree revealed Himself to the hearts of His disciples when He said to them, 'Follow me,' they would never have forsaken all immediately and followed Him. 'He manifested forth His glory,' says St John, 'and His disciples believed on Him'; and yet, when the manifestation was chiefly external, how weak was the effect it produced even upon them! How was our Lord after all obliged to upbraid them with their *unbelief*, their *little faith*, and on a particular occasion with their *having no* faith! If we know, savingly, that Jesus is 'God with us, flesh and blood', then mere man with all his best powers 'hath not revealed this to us, but our Father who is in heaven. As no man knoweth the Father save the Son, and he to whom the Son will reveal Him: so no man knoweth the Son but the Father', and he to whom the Spirit proceeding from the Father does reveal Him. 'For no man can' savingly 'say that Jesus is the Lord, but by the Holy Ghost'; and 'he that hath seen me', by this divine revelation, says Jesus, 'hath seen the Father also; for I and the Father are one.'

Had not our Lord revealed Himself in a peculiar manner to sinners, no one would have suspected Him to be 'God manifest in the flesh'. Till He discovers Himself, as He does not unto the world, 'He hath no form nor comeliness,' says Isaiah, 'and when we see Him, there is no beauty in Him, that we should desire Him; we hide as it were our faces from Him; He is despised, and we esteem Him not.' He was obliged to say to the woman of Samaria, 'I that speak unto thee am He'; and to say it with a power that penetrated her heart, before she could 'believe with her heart unto righteousness'. Then indeed, divinely wrought upon, she ran and invited her neighbours to draw living water out of the well of salvation she had so happily found.

If our Lord had not called Zaccheus inwardly as well as outwardly; if He had not made him come down from the pinnacle of proud nature, as well as from the sycomore tree; if He had not honoured his heart with His spiritual, as He did his house with His bodily presence, the rich publican would never have received Him gladly, nor would the Lord have said, 'This day is salvation come to thy house, forasmuch as thou art a son of faithful Abraham.'

Salvation did not enter into the heart of Simon, who admitted our Lord to his house and table, as well as Zaccheus. The penitent woman, who kissed His feet and washed them with her tears, obtained the blessing which the self-righteous Pharisee despised. It was to her contrite spirit, and not to his callous heart, that the Lord revealed Himself as the pardoning God.

The blind man, restored in his bodily sight, knew not his heavenly benefactor till a second and greater miracle was wrought upon the eyes of his blind understanding. When Jesus found him some time after he was cured, He said to him, 'Dost thou believe on the Son of God?' and he answered, 'Who is He, Lord, that I might believe on Him?' And Jesus, opening the eyes of his mind and manifesting Himself to him, as He does not unto the world, said, 'Thou hast both seen Him, and it is He that talketh with thee.' Then, and not till then, he could say from the heart, 'Lord, I believe'; and he worshipped Him.

Both the thieves who were crucified with Him heard His prayers and strong cries; both saw His patience and His meekness, His wounds and His blood. One continued to make sport of His sufferings, as though He had been a worse malefactor than himself; while the other, blessed with an internal revelation of His Godhead, implored His mercy, trusted Him with his soul, and confessed Him to be the King of glory, at the very moment when He hung tortured and dying as the basest of slaves.

St Peter speaks so highly of the manifestation with which he and the two sons of Zebedee were favoured on Mount Tabor, that we ought not to pass over it in silence. They saw the kingdom of God coming with power; they beheld the King in His beauty. 'His face did shine like the sun, and His raiment became white as light; a bright cloud overshadowed Him, and behold, a voice out of the cloud,' which said, 'This is my beloved Son in whom I am well pleased; hear ye Him.'

Nor did our Lord reveal Himself less after His resurrection. Mary sought Him at the grave with tears. 'As she turned herself, she saw Him standing, but knew not that it was Jesus. He said unto her, Why weepest thou? Whom seekest thou? She, supposing Him to be the gardener,' inquired after the object of her love; until Jesus, calling her by name, manifested Himself to her as alive from the dead. Then she cried out '*Master!*' and in her transport would have taken her old place at His feet.

With equal condescension He appeared to Simon, that he might not be swallowed up with over-much sorrow. True mourners in Sion weep, some for an absent God, as Mary; others for their sins as Peter; and they will not be comforted, no, not by angels, but only by Him who is nigh to all that call upon Him, and is health to those that are broken in heart. He that appeared first to weeping Mary, and next to sorrowing Peter, will shortly visit them with His salvation. He is already *with them*, as He was with Mary, though they know it not; and He will soon be *in them*, the sure and comfortable hope of glory.

This observation is further confirmed by the experience of the two disciples who walked to Emmaus, and were sad. Jesus drew near, joined and comforted them. 'He made their hearts to burn within them while He talked with them by the way, and opened to them the Scriptures. But still their eyes were held, that they should not know Him,' before they were prepared for the overwhelming favour. And it was not until He sat at meat with them that 'their eyes were opened, and they knew Him' in the breaking of bread. By a fatal mistake many professors in our day rest satisfied with what did not satisfy the two disciples. They understood the Scriptures, their hearts burnt with love and joy; Jesus was with them, but they knew Him not until the happy moment when He fully opened the eyes of their faith, and poured the light of His countenance on their ravished spirits. Happy those who, like them, constrain an unknown Jesus by mighty prayers to tarry with them until the veil is taken away from their hearts and they 'know in whom they have believed'.

Frequent were the manifestations of Jesus to His disciples before His ascension. An angel appeared to two of the holy mourners, and said to them, 'Fear not; for I know that ye seek Jesus, who was crucified. He is risen from the dead.' As they ran with fear and great joy to tell His disciples, Jesus met them saying, 'All hail!' and they came, held Him by the feet, and worshipped Him. The same day in the evening, when the doors were shut where the disciples were assembled for fear of the Jews, came Jesus, and stood in the midst. They were terrified, but with His wonted goodness He said, 'Peace be unto you!' He showed them His hands and His feet, ate with them as He had done of old with Abraham; and, to testify an inward manifestation of the Holy Ghost which He imparted to them, breathed upon them, as His Spirit breathed upon their minds; and thus 'He opened their understandings that they might understand the Scriptures'. Out of condescension to Thomas, He showed Himself to them a second time, in the like manner; and a third time at the sea of Tiberias: and 'afterward He was seen of above five hundred brethren at once'.

You will perhaps say that these manifestations ceased when Christ was ascended to heaven. This is true with respect to the manifestations of a body of such gross flesh and blood as may be touched with material hands. In this sense believers 'know Christ after the flesh no more'. Our Lord, by His gentle reproof to Thomas, discountenanced our looking for carnal manifestations of His person, and they are not what I contend for. But that spiritual manifestations of Christ ceased at His ascension is what I must deny, if I receive the Scripture. On the contrary, they become more frequent. Three thousand were 'pricked to the heart' on the day of Pentecost, and felt the need of a visit from the heavenly Physician. He then came revealed in the power of His Spirit, with whom He is one. They received the gift of the Holy Ghost, whose office it is to manifest the Son. For 'the promise was unto them and their children, and as many as the Lord our God shall call'; witness the last words of Christ in St Matthew's Gospel, 'Lo, I am with you alway, even unto the end of the world.'

Time would fail me to tell of the 5,000 converted some days after, of Cornelius and his household, Lydia and her household; in a word, of all who were truly brought to Christ in the first age of Christianity. The Lord 'opened their hearts. The Holy Ghost fell upon them; and they walked in His comforts'. Christ was evidently set forth crucified before their spiritual eyes. He dwelt in their hearts by faith: they lived not, but Christ lived in them. They agreed with St Paul in saying, 'If any man have not the Spirit of Christ', by whom He is savingly known, 'he is none of His'.

Stephen's experience is alone sufficient to decide this point. When brought before the council, *they all saw his face as it had been the face of an angel.* Being *full of the Holy Ghost,* he wrought no miracle, he spake no new tongue; but 'looked steadfastly up into heaven, and saw the glory of God, and Jesus standing at the right hand of God'. This manifestation was calculated only for the private encouragement and comfort of the pious deacon. It answered no other end but to enrage the Jews, and make them account him a greater blasphemer and a wilder enthusiast than they did before. Accordingly they cried aloud, stopped their ears, ran upon him, cast him out of the city, and stoned him; while Stephen, under the powerful influence of the manifestation, 'kneeled down, called upon God, saying, Lord Jesus, receive my spirit, and lay not this sin to their charge'. Hence we learn, first, that nothing appears so absurd and wicked to Pharisees and formalists, as the doctrine I maintain. They lose all patience when they hear that Christ really manifests Himself to His servants. No blasphemy is like this in the account of those who are wise, learned, and prudent in their own eyes. Secondly, that the most exalted saints need a fresh manifestation of the glory, love, and presence of Christ, that they may depart this life in the triumph of faith.

If you object, that Stephen was thus favoured because he was about to suffer for Christ, and that it would be great presumption to expect the like support, I reply in five following observations. 1. We are called to suffer for Christ, as well as Stephen, though perhaps not in the same manner and degree. 2. We often need as much support from Christ to stand against the children of men that are 'set on fire, whose teeth are spears and arrows, and their tongues a sharp sword; and to quench the fiery darts of the devil' as the martyr did to stand a shower of stones. 3. It is perhaps as hard to be racked with the gout, or to burn several days in a fever on a sick bed, as you or I may be forced to do, as to be for a few minutes with Shadrach and his companions in a burning furnace, or to feel for a fleeting moment the anguish of bruised flesh and a fractured skull, with our triumphant martyr. No one knows what pangs of body and agonies of soul may accompany him through the valley of the shadow of death. If our Lord Himself was not above being strengthened by an angel that appeared to Him from heaven, surely it is no enthusiasm to say that such feeble creatures as we are stand in need of a divine manifestation, to enable us to fight our last battle manfully, and to come off more than conquerors. 4. We betray unbelief if we suppose that Christ cannot do for us what He did for Stephen; and we betray our presumption if we say we want not the assistance which this bold champion stood in need of. 5. The language of our church is far different: 'Grant,' she says, in her collect for that saint's day, 'O Lord, that in all our sufferings here on earth for the testimony of Thy truth, we may steadfastly look up to heaven, and by faith behold the glory that shall be revealed; and being filled with the Holy Ghost, may learn to love and bless our persecutors, by the example of the first martyr, St Stephen, who prayed for his murderers, O blessed Jesus, who standest at the right hand of God, to succour all those who suffer for Thee.'

But suppose you reject the testimony of St Stephen, and of all our clergy (when in the desk) touching the reality, and the necessity too, of our Lord manifesting Himself on earth after His ascension into heaven, receive at least that of St Luke and St Paul. They both inform us that as Saul of Tarsus went to Damascus, 'the Lord, even Jesus, appeared to him in the way. Suddenly there shone a light from heaven above the brightness of the sun, so that he fell on the earth, and heard a voice saying, Saul, Saul, why persecutest thou me?' And he said, 'Who art Thou, Lord?' And the Lord said, 'I am Jesus, whom thou persecutest.' So powerful was the effect of this manifestation of Christ, that the sinner was turned into a saint, and the fierce, blaspheming persecutor into a weeping, praying apostle.

Methinks I hear you say, True, into an apostle; but are we called to be apostles? No, but we are called to be Christians, to be converted from sin to holiness, and from the kingdom of darkness to the kingdom of God's dear Son. St Paul's call to the apostleship is nothing to his being made a child of God. Judas was a Christian by profession, an apostle by call, and *devil* by nature. And what is Judas in his own place to the meanest of God's children, to poor Lazarus in Abraham's bosom? All who go to heaven are first 'turned from darkness to light, and from the power of Satan unto God'. This turning sometimes begins by a manifestation of Christ; witness the authentic account of Colonel Gardner's conversion, published by his judicious friend, Dr Doddridge; and the more authentic one of our apostle's conversion recorded three times by St Luke. And I dare to advance, upon the authority of One greater than St Luke, that no one's conversion ever was completed without the revelation of the Son of God to his heart. 'I am the way and the door,' says Jesus, 'no man comes to the Father but by me.' 'Look unto me and be ye saved, all ye ends of the earth.' Our looking to Him for salvation would be to as little purpose were He not to manifest Himself to us, as our looking towards the east for light if the sun were not to rise upon us.

The revelation of Christ, productive of St Paul's conversion, was not the only one with which the apostle was favoured. At Corinth the Lord encouraged and spake to him in the night by a vision. 'Be not afraid, but speak and hold not thy peace; for I am with thee, and no man shall hurt thee.' On another occasion, to wean him more from earth, Christ favoured him with the nearest views of heaven. 'I knew a man in Christ,' says he, 'whether in the body or out of the body I cannot tell, who was caught up into the third heaven, into Paradise, and heard words which it is not possible for man to utter.' And, he informs us further, that 'lest he should be exalted above measure through the abundance of the revelations, a messenger of Satan was suffered to buffet him'. When he had been brought before the Sanhedrim for preaching the Gospel, St Luke informs us that 'the night following the Lord stood by him, and said, "Be of good cheer, Paul; for as thou hast testified of me in Jerusalem, so must thou bear witness also at Rome".' The ship in which he sailed being endangered by a storm, there stood by him 'the angel of God, whose he was, and whom he served, saying, Fear not Paul . . .'

St Paul was not the only one to whom Christ manifested Himself in His familiar manner. Ananias of Damascus was neither an apostle nor a deacon: nevertheless to him 'said the Lord in a vision, Ananias. And he said, Behold, I am here, Lord; and the Lord said, Arise, and go into the street which is called Straight, and enquire in the house of Judas for one called Saul of Tarsus: for, behold, he prayeth.' In like manner Philip was directed to go near and join himself to the eunuch's chariot. And St Peter, being informed that three men sought him, the Lord said to him, 'Arise and go with them, doubting nothing; for I have sent them.'

Whether we place these manifestations in the class of the extraordinary, or of the mixt ones, we equally learn from them. First, that the Lord Jesus revealed Himself as much after His ascension as He did before. Secondly, that if He does it to send His servants with a Gospel message to particular persons, He will do it much more to make that message effectual, and to bring salvation to those that wait for Him.

As for the revelations of Christ to St John, they were so many that the last book of the New Testament is called the Revelation, as containing chiefly an account of them. 'I was in the Spirit on the Lord's day,' says the apostle, 'and I heard behind me a great voice, as of a trumpet, saying, I am the first and the last. I turned to see the voice that spake with me, and I saw one like unto the Son of man . . . When I saw Him, I fell at His feet as dead: and He laid His hand upon me, saying, Fear not; I am the first and the last. Write the things which are and shall be.' One of the things which our Lord commanded John to write is a most glorious promise, that *He stands at the door* of the human heart, ready to manifest Himself even to poor lukewarm Laodiceans; and that *if any man hear His voice and open the door*, if they are conscious of their need of Him so as to open their hearts by the prayer of faith, *He will come in*, and feast them with His gracious presence, and the delicious fruits of His blessed Spirit. Therefore the most extraordinary of all the revelations, that of St John in Patmos, not only shews that the manifestations of Christ run parallel in the canon of Scripture, but also give a peculiar sanction to the ordinary revelations of Him for which I contend.

I conclude by two inferences, which appear to me undeniable. The first, that it is evident our Lord before His incarnation, during His stay on earth, and after His ascension into heaven, hath been pleased in a variety of manners to manifest Himself to the children of men, both for the benefit of the church in general, and for the conversion of sinners, and for the establishment of saints in particular. Secondly, that the doctrine I maintain is as old as Adam, as modern as St John, the last of the inspired writers, and as Scriptural as the Old and New Testament, which is what I wanted to demonstrate.

ANDREW ALEXANDER BONAR (1810-1892)

Reared in, and ordained to the ministry of the Church of Scotland, the brothers Horatius and Andrew Bonar both joined the Free Church at the disruption of 1843; both attained eminence as preachers and as writers — Horatius, especially as a hymn-writer; and both received the honorary degree of Doctor of Divinity — Horatius from Aberdeen University, and Andrew from Edinburgh. Both were close friends of Robert Murray McCheyne, who was Andrew's assistant for a year when licensed to preach in 1835. Andrew fulfilled a notable ministry at Finnieston Church, Glasgow, from 1856 until his death in 1892, and was Moderator of the Free Church General Assembly in 1878. His *Memoir and Remains* of McCheyne — posthumously published letters and sermons — became a 'classic' almost immediately; as did his *Memoir and Letters of Samuel Rutherford*. He wrote scholarly commentaries on Leviticus and the Psalms; but our selected extract is taken from a little book entitled *The Gospel Pointing to the Person of Christ*, published in 1852.

LOOKING TO THE PERSON OF CHRIST

No one could be supposed to have seen the Alps if he tells you that all he saw was some rocky ridges of hills, which his eye felt no strain in looking to. The Alps are not such hills; they tower to the clouds. Equally true it is that no one can be considered as having seen sin really, who never saw it to be very great; or to have got real rest to his soul, who has not seen the Saviour to be very great. Indeed, very great salvation is needed in order to give any true peace to a soul truly awakened; such salvation as is discovered when the soul discovers the Person of the Saviour. Then it sings, *'Jah Jehovah* is my strength and song, and has become my salvation' (Isa 12. 2). 'In *Jah Jehovah* is the Rock of ages' (26. 4). (These are the only passages where that particular combination occurs, *Jah Jehovah*, as if to gather up the fullness of Godhead-existence in one clause, when singing of Him who is our salvation. He is mine, from whom every drop of being came!)

Even one sin makes peace flee from the soul, as we see in the case of Adam and Eve. Even one sin fills the soul with suspicions of God and suggestions of fear. Of course, then, the conscience of every sinner abounds in materials for fear before God. Achan may be secure for a time, while his wedge of gold and his Babylonish garment remain hid in the tent; but let a hurricane from the howling wilderness shake the cords and canvas of his tent, and threaten to blow aside the covering of his theft, and then he is full of alarm! Now, every sin is, to the conscience of the sinner, like Achan's theft. There may be a present calm in the air, but who can promise that there shall not arise a stormy wind, a hurricane threatening to tear up the stakes of his earthly tabernacle? Who can engage that every sin shall not be laid bare? Who can give security that the sinner shall not very speedily be sisted (summoned) at the bar of the Holy One? It is a small matter to say that at present all is at rest within. A city may be wrapt in slumber, and under the calm moon may seem quiet as a cemetery; and yet the first beams of the morning sun may awake the sleeping rebels, and witness the burst of revolutionary frenzy.

Every sin is secretly uttering to the man God's sentence of death; insinuating uneasy forebodings regarding coming wrath. Every sin mutters to the sinner something more or less distinct about having wronged God, and about God being too holy and just to let it slip from remembrance. And when the quickening Spirit is at work in the conscience, every sin begins to cry loudly to the Lord for vengeance against him in whose heart it has its abode.

For such a state of soul only one thing can avail—the discovery (which the Spirit makes to the man in conversion), of Christ's full sacrifice for sin. Therein may be seen a propitiation as full and efficacious as conscience craves, because it is the work of Him who is Godman. Therein may be seen the *whole person of the Saviour*, presented to the soul as the object to be embraced, and that person associated with the merit of all He has done and suffered. Nay, more; every act and suffering of that glorious Person confronts the case of every sinner. Not only does He remedy the case of every individual sinner in all that 'multitude which no man can number', but besides, He meets *every individual sin*, and applies outpoured life to every stain, to blot it out. This is exactly what is needed. To see Him who is the atonement as Godman, is to see an offering so vast, and full of applications so wide, that every crevice of the conscience must be reached.

He is our peace, not by His death only, but by His life of obedience, imputed to us; the more therefore we go into details with *His person* (whose every act and agony has an infinite capability of application, because He is the Godman), then the more shall we feel good reason for our peace through Him, 'passing understanding' (Phil. 4.7). Let us exhibit some details of the kind we refer to. His personal acts and sufferings meeting my personal disobedience, and my personal desert of wrath.

I confess the sin of *my nature*, my original sin: 'Behold, I was shapen in iniquity, and in sin did my mother conceive me' (Psa. 51.5). But I see in Christ one who was 'that Holy One', born to be holiness to others (Luke 1.25). His *dying* was fully sufficient to remove the guilt of my conception, and my connection with Adam; while His *doing* was holy from the womb. Behold, then, here am I in my substitute! My infancy without iniquity, nay, with actual purity, in the eye of Him who is well pleased with my substitute.

I confess the sin of my *childhood*. My childhood and youth were vanity. But I find in Christ, Godman and my substitute, deliverance from all this. 'The *child* grew and waxed strong in spirit, filled with wisdom; and the grace of God was upon Him' (Luke 2.40). I get all the positive merit of this childhood of my surety; full as it was of holy wisdom, and free from every taint of folly and thoughtlessness; and along with this I get the atoning merit of His death. And then I present to God both satisfaction for the trespasses I have done in childhood, and also obedience equivalent in full to what the law even then demanded of me.

I confess more particularly the sin of my *thoughts*. 'The imagination of the thoughts of my heart have been only evil continually' (Gen. 6.5). But I discover Him who not only could say that by death He had perfected the atonement for me, but who also obeyed my obedience in the thoughts of His heart, saying, 'Thy law is within my heart' ('in midst of my bowels'). Psa. 40.8.

I confess the sin of my *words*, my idle words, my evil words (Matt. 12.36). But I find in this great atonement the penalty paid for my every idle word; and at the same time, the rendering of the obedience due, inasmuch as His mouth was a well of life, 'grace was poured into His lips' (Psa. 45.2) and men never heard Him utter ought but holiness.

I confess the sin of my *duties*. But if it be the sin of my careless *worship* in the sanctuary, I find my glorious substitute worshipping for me in the synagogue (Luke 4.16) and vindicating the honour of His Father in the temple-service (John 2.17). His songs of praise, His deep attention to the written Word then read, His joining in the public prayers, all this He puts to my account, as if I had done it, and done it always—while He also blots out every accusation to the contrary by His blood.

I confess my *prayerlessness* in secret. It has grieved the Lord to the heart. But I find my surety 'rising a great while before day, and departing to a solitary place to pray' (Mark 1.35), or 'continuing all night in prayer to God' (Luke 6.12). This He will impute to me, as if I had prayed every day and night; at the same time plunging my sins of omission into the depths of the sea.

I confess and deplore *heart-sins* of various kinds. I lament instability of soul; my goodness is like the early dew. But He was 'the same yesterday, today, and for ever', both God-ward and man-ward (Heb. 13.8). I feel *hardness* of heart. But He imputes to me His own tenderness, and reckons to my account His yearnings of soul for the glory of His Father. I am *stubborn*; but He can say, 'The Lord God hath opened mine ear, and I was not rebellious, neither turned away backwards' (Isa. 50.5). In me is *guile;* but 'In His mouth was no guile found' (1 Peter 2.22). And thus there is not only ready the warp of satisfaction for transgression, but also the woof of rendered obedience.

Let me still go on a little in this application of my Lord's active and passive righteousness. Do I feel my soul in anguish, because of indulging *ambitious projects*, seeking to be somewhat? I find Him, 'not seeking His own glory' (John 8.50), and this fold of His robe He will cast over me, while He washes me from my self-seeking in His blood.

I have *pleased* myself. But of Him it is testified, 'He pleased not Himself' (Rom. 15.3). I have sought my own *will*. But He could declare before the Father and to men, 'I seek not mine own will, but the will of my Father which hath sent me' (John 5.30). And thus has He the very form of obedience that I have omitted to render. He gave what I withheld; and He will give it for me, at the same time hiding my guilt in withholding it, in His blood.

I have been *worldly*. I have loved 'the world and the things that are in the world' (1 John 2.15), not only the objects it presents, but the very place itself, in preference to where the direct presence of God might be enjoyed. But He did not. 'He was not of the world' (John 17:16). He never had any of its treasure; it is doubtful if He ever possessed or handled any of its money; He had, we are sure, no where to lay His head. The world hated Him, 'because He testified that the works thereof were evil' (John 7.7). And thus He has that to impute to me, while He washes me from guilt.

I have been often *double-minded*. His eye was always single. 'I have glorified Thee' (John 17.4) was always true of Him. I have been *inconsistent*. But even Satan could 'find nothing in Him' (John 14.30). And he could challenge His foes, 'which of you convinceth me of sin?' (John 8.46). My *pride* and *haughtiness* have much need of one who was 'meek and lowly', and such I find in Him; and I find Him calling me to come to Him as such, and use Him (Matt. 11.29).

If I have *backslidden*, my surety's course was truly like 'the shining light, that shineth more and more unto the perfect day' (Prov. 4.18). 'He increased in wisdom and stature, and in favour with God and man' (Luke 2.52). Instead of *lukewarmness* even once appearing in Him, at one time such was His zeal for man's salvation that friends stood by and said, 'He is beside Himself' (Mark 3.21); and at another, His disciples were irresistibly led back to the words of the psalmist, 'the zeal of Thine house hath eaten me up' (John 2.17). Now, all this active righteousness in Him is for my use. He will throw over me this other fold of His robe, as well as apply His infinitely precious death — and thus no one shall ever be able to accuse me of backsliding, acknowledging my surety's worth for me.

I have *grieved the Spirit*. But oh, how Christ honoured Him! Such blessed things He said of Him! 'The Comforter', 'The Spirit of truth', 'The Holy Spirit' were names applied to Him; and Himself had been led by the Spirit (Matt. 4.1) in delighted acquiescence. He has something here also to present instead of my provocations; and what He has, He will use for me. Only let me know the treasures hid in His Person, and my consolation must abound.

I have been *unthankful*; but oh! how my surety aboundeth in thanksgivings — thanksgivings for food; thanksgivings for the Gospel to babes; thanksgivings for the communion table, because it proclaimed His dying for us. Herein I find obedience to the law I broke, the law of gratitude, while in the sacrifice of Calvary I find expiation for its guilt.

I think upon my *unconcern for souls*, and find the only remedy for that iniquity in Him whose heart burned 'to seek and to save that which was lost', and who plunged into the sea of wrath in order to redeem; for every step in His atonement has in it something of obedience as well as satisfaction.

Oh, the inconceivable fullness for us in Him, whatever the special sin which our conscience may at any moment be feeling. Only let us ever keep *Christ Himself* in view, Christ clothed to the foot in that garment of active and passive righteousness. It is thus we get the sea, with all its multitudinous waves (Isa. 48.18) to flow up every creek and sweep around every bay. [There is also a wave of it for *ministerial* failures: for He never failed, but could appeal to His Father, 'I have declared Thy faithfulness, and Thy salvation' (Psa. 40.9–10). His Shepherd's heart and work covers over ours. And so let a *teacher* repair to Him for the hiding of sins in teaching: Luke 21.37; John 18.20] His *person* being such, all His work fits into the soul's necessities. And all this is so great that not only does it affect us *negatively* — not only does this full view of Christ remove every tremor from the soul — but it works into the heart with *positive* bestowal of bliss.

It is, as sometimes in nature, when every breath of wind is so lulled asleep that not a leaf moves on the bough of any tree; the sun is shedding his parting ray on the still foliage; and the sea rests as if it had become a pavement of crystal. This is peace in nature. Your heart feels, amid such a scene, not only the absence of whatsoever might create alarm or disquiet, but the presence of some elements of positive enjoyment, as if there were an infusion of bliss in the scene. Now it is infinitely more so in the kingdom of grace. The presence of *Christ* in the heart (the Spirit there testifying of *Christ Himself*) lulls fear to sleep, and makes disquiet almost an impossibility; but further, it brings positive delight and bliss. There is something in it to '*keep* the heart and mind' (*garrison*, and so preserve secure). What can this positive element be, but the real outbreathing of direct

friendship and love from Him whose heart we now know? He removes
the barriers thoroughly, in order to bring in Himself with all His
love—Himself rich in all the affections and bowels of mercy. And is
not this the true 'healing' of the 'hurt'? Was not the 'hurt', our
separation from the Holy One, caused by sin? Is not this the 'healing'
—our return to *fellowship with Him?*

It is worth while asking, in every case of apparent peace, whether
or not this *positive* element exists. Is there not only the absence of
dread and a calmness in looking toward the Holy One, but is there
also a direct enjoyment of Him who gives the peace? The work of
Christ, if seen apart from His Person, may give freedom from dread
and wrath, but it can scarcely impart that positive delight in His
restored friendship which alone 'keepeth the heart and mind'.

. 'He is our peace,' says Paul (Ephes. 2.14). And when, in Philippians 4.7 he spoke of His peace keeping the heart and mind (the
thoughts, in the original), he said it was 'by Christ Jesus'. Was not
Paul directed by the Spirit here to insert this clause in order to fix our
eye on *the Person* who is *our peace*—the true 'Jehovah-shalom'
(Judges 6.24)? And is not the reason of this to be found in the fact
that in the proportion as we see *the Person*, our soul's peace deepens
and spreads? Certainly, all who have ever tried it find this to be the
case. The more they know of Him, the more complete is their souls'
rest. It is a shallow peace, if indeed it be the 'peace of God' at all,
when the person of the Peace-maker is not directly realized.

And now, seeing we have such advantages above Old Testament
saints, who saw *the Person* so dimly, are there not duties and
responsibilities resulting? 'The darkness is past and the true light now
shineth' (1 John 2.8). Therefore (says John), there is for you *a new
commandment*. He seems to mean that the increase of light gave
force to every demand for obedience; and specially that the appearing of *this Light*, the Person of Jesus, brought with it peculiar
motives to obedience. May we not say that if we get such peace in
Jesus Christ, and have Himself to calm our souls, the Lord may well
expect at our hands a higher style of obedience than in former days?

Peace has its responsibilities—such peace, through such a
Redeemer, has no common responsibilities. We are freed from
burdens in order to work for God; fully justified in order to be the
more fully sanctified. Carry this kind of peace with you everywhere,
and you cannot fail everywhere to show that you are with Jesus; for it
is *Himself realized* that gives it. Your claim to real peace implies your
seeing *Christ Himself*, and enjoying His fellowship. If so, then you
may well be expected to show likeness to Jesus; for 'He that walketh

with the wise shall be wise' (Prov. 13.20). Your peace will be characterized by purity, as all is that comes from God (James 3.17), and as all must be that is the direct effect of your eye fixed on 'God manifest in the flesh'. Your peace 'in Jesus Christ' will keep you daily at His side, engaged in His work, guided by His eye, satisfied with His smile, living to do His will. Who could have his eye on the Saviour continually in order to see 'peace in heaven' toward himself, and yet at the same time turn his feet into the byepaths of unholiness?

Were your peace gotten or maintained by looking at an *act* of your own, viz, your having once believed, or having done the thing called believing, then possibly you might be at peace and yet not walk with God. But inasmuch as true Scriptural peace is gotten and maintained by the sinner's eye resting at the moment on *the Person of Him* who is our peace—on the Person of Jehovah-shalom—it is not possible to be at peace and yet willingly wander from fellowship with the Holy One. Christ, our Peace-maker, walks wherever is to be found anything 'true, or honest, or just, or lovely, or of good report', wherever is to be seen 'any virtue or any praise' (Phil. 4.8). And he who has peace by having his eye on Christ cannot enjoy this peace without being led at the same moment to these walks of Christ. Hence it is that Paul writes to the Philippian church—to Lydia and the jailor, and Euodias and Syntyche, and Clement—that 'the God of peace would be with them' while they pursued these objects (Phil. 4. 8–9). If they were found at any time wandering from these holy paths, it would be sufficient sign to them (as it will be to us also) that they had for the time taken off their eyes from *Him* who was their peace; and so, ereever (*sic*) they were aware, they lost the enjoyment of that deep, profound peace, which 'keepeth the heart and mind'.

ROBERT MURRAY McCHEYNE (1813-1843)

In his short life of 30 years, Robert Murray McCheyne became widely known as a man of saintly character, whose preaching deeply moved his congregation at St Peter's (Church of Scotland), Dundee, and effected a spiritual transformation akin to revival in the town. 'Few ministers have so greatly influenced their own and succeeding generations in so short a life,' the *Dictionary of the Christian Church* observes. That continuing influence has been exercised pre-eminently through the *Memoir and Remains of Robert Murray McCheyne*, edited by his intimate friend, Andrew Bonar'. This sermon, undated, is characteristic of his expository, allegorical style.

'MY SISTER, MY SPOUSE'

The name given to believers in Song of Solomon 4.12 is 'my sister, my spouse', or rather, 'my sister-spouse'. There are many sweet names from the lips of Christ addressed to believers: 'O thou fairest among women' (1.8); 'My love' (2.2); 'My love, my fair one' (2.10); 'O my dove' (2.14); 'My sister, my love, my dove, my undefiled' (5.2); 'O prince's daughter' (7.1). But here is one more tender than all, *'My sister, my spouse'* (4.9); and again, verse 10, and here, verse 12. To be spoken well of by the world is little to be desired; but to hear Christ speak such words to us is enough to fill our hearts with heavenly joy. The meaning you will see by what Paul says: 'Have we not power to lead about a sister, a wife, as well as other apostles?' (1 Cor. 9.5). He means power to marry one who is likeminded—a sister in the Lord; one who will be both a wife and a sister in Christ Jesus: *a wife* by covenant, *a sister* by being born of the same Father in heaven. So Christ here says of believers, 'My sister, my spouse', that they are not only united to Him by choice and covenant, but are likeminded also.

1. THESE TWO THINGS ARE INSEPARABLE. Some would like to be *the spouse* of the Saviour, without being the sister. Some would like to be saved by Christ, but not to be made like Christ. When Christ chooses a sinner, and sets His love on the soul, and when He woos the soul and draws it into covenant with Himself, it is only that He may make the soul a sister, that He may impart His features, His same heart, His all, to the soul. Now, many rest in the mere forgiveness of sins. Many have felt Christ wooing their soul, and offering Himself freely to them, and they have accepted Him. They have consented to the match. Sinful and worthless and hell-deserving, they find that Christ desires it; that He will not be dishonoured by it; that He will find glory in it; and their heart is filled with joy in being taken into covenant with so glorious a bridegroom. But why has He done it? To make you partaker of His holiness, to change your nature, to make you sister to Himself, of His own mind and spirit. He has sprinkled you with clean water, only that He may give you a new heart also. He brings you to Himself and gives you rest only that He may make you learn of Him His meekness and lowliness in heart.

(i) You cannot be the spouse of Christ without becoming sister also. Christ offers to be the bridegroom of sin-covered souls. He came from heaven for this; took flesh and blood for this. He tries to woo sinners, standing and stretching out His hands. He tells them of His power and glory and riches, and that all shall be theirs. He is a blood-besprinkled bridegroom; but that is His chief loveliness. The soul believes His Word, melts under His love, consents to be His. 'My beloved is mine, and I am His.' Then He washes the soul in His own blood; clothes it in His own righteousness; takes it in with Him to the presence of His Father. From that day the soul begins to reflect His image. Christ begins to live in the soul. The same heart, the same spirit, are in both. The soul becomes sister as well as spouse — Christ's not only by choice and covenant, but by likeness also. Some of you Christ has chosen; you have become His justified ones. Do you rest there? No; remember you must be made like Him, reflect His image; you cannot separate the two.

(ii) *The order of the two.* You must be first the spouse, before you can be the sister of Christ; His by covenant before His by likeness. Some think to be like Christ first, that they will copy His features till they recommend themselves to Christ. No, this will not do. He chooses only those that have no comeliness — polluted in their own blood, that He may have the honour of washing them. 'When thou wast in thy blood' (Ezek. 16.6). Are there any trying to recommend themselves to Christ by their change of life? Oh, how little you know Him! He comes to seek those who are black in themselves. Are there some of you poor, defiled, unclean? You are just the soul Christ woos. Proud, scornful? Christ woos you. He offers you His all, and then He will change you.

2. To what Christ compares believers:

(i) *'A garden enclosed'.* The gardens in the East are always enclosed; sometimes by a fence of reeds, such are the gardens of cucumbers in the wilderness; sometimes by a stone wall, as the garden of Gethsemane; sometimes by a hedge of prickly pear. But what is still more interesting is, they are often enclosed out of a wilderness. All around is often barren sand; and this one enclosed spot is like the garden of the Lord. Such is the believer.

Enclosed by election. In the eye of God the world was one great wilderness, all barren, all dead, all fruitless. No part was fit to bear anything but briers. It was nigh unto cursing. One part was no better than another in His sight. The hearts of men were all as hard as rock, dry and barren as the sand. Out of the mere good pleasure of His will

He marked out a garden of delights where He might show His power and grace, that it might be to His praise. Some of you know your election of God by the fruits of it, by your faith, love, and holiness. Be humbled by the thought that it was solely because He chose you. Why me, Lord, why me?

Enclosed by the Spirit's work. Election is the planning of the garden. The Spirit's work is the carrying it into effect. 'He fenced it' (Isa. 5.2). When the Spirit begins His work it is separating work. When a man is convinced of sin he is no more one with the careless, godless world. He avoids his companions, goes alone. When a soul comes to Christ it is still more separated. It then comes into a new world. He is no more under the curse; no more under wrath. He is in the smile and favour of God. Like Gideon's fleece, he now receives the dew when all around is dry.

Enclosed by the arms of God. God is a wall of fire. Angels are around the soul. Elisha's hill was full of horses of fire. God is round about the soul, as the mountains stand round about Jerusalem. The soul is hid in the secret of God's presence. No robber can ever come over the fence. 'A vineyard of red wine: I the Lord do keep it; I will water it every moment: lest any hurt it, I will keep it night and day' (Isa. 27.2–3). This is sung over thee.

An Eastern garden was watered in three ways: by a hidden well — it is the custon in the East to roll a stone over the mouth of a well, to preserve the water from sand; by a fountain of living water — a well always bubbling up; by streams from Lebanon.

(ii) *'A spring shut up'.* This describes the Spirit in the heart, in His most secret manner of working. In some gardens there is only this secret well. A stone is over the mouth. If you wish to water the garden you must roll away the stone, and let down the bucket. Such is the life of God in many souls. Some of you feel that there is a stone over the mouth of the well in you. Your own rocky heart is the stone. Stir up the gift of God which is in thee.

(iii) *A well of living water.* This is the same as John 4 — a well that is ever full and ever running over. Grace new every moment; fresh upspringings from God. Thus only will you advance.

(iv) *Streams from Lebanon.* These are very plentiful. On all sides they fall in pleasant cascades, in the bottom unite into broad, full streams, and on their way water the richest gardens. So believers are sometimes favoured with streams from the Lebanon that is above. We receive out of Christ's fullness; drink of the wine of His pleasures. Oh, for more of these streams of Lebanon! Even in the dry season they are full. The hotter the summer, the streams from Lebanon become the fuller, because the heat only melts the mountain snows.

3. THE FRUIT. The very use of a garden is to bear fruit and flowers.
For this purpose it is enclosed, hedged, planted, watered. If it bear
no fruit nor flowers, all the labour is lost labour. The ground is nigh
to cursing. So it is with the Christian. Three remarkable things are
here:

(i) *No weeds are mentioned.* Pleasant fruit trees, and all the chief
spices; but no weeds. Had it been a man that was describing his
garden, he would have begun with the weeds—the unbelief,
corruption, evil tempers, etc. Not so Christ. He covers all the sins.
The weeds are lost sight of. He sees no perversity. As in John 17:6,
'They have kept Thy word; they are not of the world.' As in
Revelation 2.2, 'I know thy works.'

(ii) *The fruit was the very best—the pomegranate.* All were
pleasant fruits, and all His own. 'From me is thy fruit found'; 'His
pleasant fruits' (v. 16). The graces that Christ puts into the heart and
brings out of the life are the very best, the richest, most pleasant,
most excellent that a creature can produce. Love to Christ, love to
the brethren, love to the Sabbath, forgiveness of enemies, all the best
fruits that can grow in the human heart. Unreasonable world, to
condemn true conversion, when it produces the very fruits of
paradise, acceptable to God, if not to you. Should not this make you
stand and consider?

(iii) *There were spices in this garden.* These spices do not
naturally grow in gardens. Even in the East there never was such a
display as this. So the fragrant graces of the Spirit are not natural to
the heart. They are brought from a far country. They must be
carefully watched. They need the stream, and the gentle zephyr. Oh,
I fear most of you should hang your heads when Christ begins to
speak of fragrant spices in your heart! Where are they? Are there not
talkative, forward Christians? Are there not self-seeking, praise-
seeking, man-pleasing Christians? Are there not proud-praying
Christians? Are there not ill-tempered Christians? Are there not rash,
inconsiderate ones? Are there not idle, lazy, bad-working Christians?
Lord, where are the spices? Verily, Christ is a bundle of myrrh. Oh to
be like Him! Oh that every flower and fruit would grow! They must
come from above. Many there are of whom one is forced to say,
'Well, they may be Christians; but I would not like to be next them in
heaven!' Cry for the wind: 'Awake, O north wind; and come, thou
south; blow upon my garden, that the spices thereof may flow out.'

JOHN C. RYLE (1816–1900)

The first Bishop of the (then) newly-formed diocese of Liverpool, John C. Ryle was an acknowledged leader of the Evangelical party in the Church of England. Educated at Eton and Christ Church, Oxford, he was a fine athlete, playing cricket and rowing for his university; he also took a first class degree in Modern Greats. He turned his back on an academic career, however, when offered a college fellowship; was ordained in 1842, serving several country parishes until his elevation to the episcopate in 1880. He was a prolific writer of tracts and pamphlets, and of his several books, *Knots Untied* was perhaps the most popular in his own day; but *Holiness* has proved the most enduring, being still in regular demand. From it we reproduce part of the chapter on 'Unsearchable Riches'.

'UNSEARCHABLE RICHES'

St Paul calls the great subject of his preaching, *The unsearchable riches of Christ* (Eph. 3.8). That the converted man of Tarsus should preach '*Christ*' is no more than we might expect from his antecedents. Having found peace through the blood of the cross himself, we may be sure he would always tell the story of the cross to others. He never wasted precious time in exalting a mere rootless morality, in descanting on vague abstractions and empty platitudes—such as 'the true', and 'the noble', and 'the earnest', and 'the beautiful', and 'the germs of goodness in human nature', and the like. He always went to the root of the matter, and showed men their great family disease, their desperate state as sinners, and the Great Physician needed by a sin-sick world.

That he should preach Christ among '*the Gentiles*', again is in keeping with all we know of his line of action in all places and among all people. Wherever he travelled and stood up to preach—at Antioch, at Lystra, at Philippi, at Athens, at Corinth, at Ephesus, among Greeks or Romans, among learned or unlearned, among Stoics and Epicureans, before rich or poor, barbarians, Scythians, bond or free—Jesus and His vicarious death, Jesus and His resurrection, was the keynote of his sermons. Varying his mode of address according to his audience, as he wisely did, the pith and heart of his preaching was Christ crucified.

But in the text before us, you will observe, he uses a very peculiar expression, an expression which unquestionably stands alone in his writings—'the unsearchable riches of Christ'. It is the strong, burning language of one who always remembered his debt to Christ's mercy and grace, and loved to show how intensely he felt it by his words. St Paul was not a man to act or speak by halves. He never forgot the road to Damascus, the house of Judas in the street called Straight, the visit of good Ananias, the scales falling from his eyes, and his own marvellous passage from death to life. These things are always fresh and green before his mind; and so he is not content to say, 'Grace is given me to preach Christ'. No: he amplifies his subject. He calls it 'the unsearchable riches of Christ'.

But what did the apostle mean when he spoke of 'unsearchable riches'? This is a hard question to answer. No doubt he saw in Christ such a boundless provision for all the wants of man's soul that he knew no other phrase to convey his meaning. From whatever standpoint he beheld Jesus, he saw in Him far more than mind could conceive, or tongue could tell. What he precisely intended must necessarily be matter of conjecture. But it may be useful to set down in detail some of the things which most probably were in his mind. It *may*, it *must*, it *ought* to be useful. For after all, let us remember, these *'riches of Christ'* are riches which you and I need in England just as much as St Paul; and, best of all, these *'riches'* are treasured up in Christ for you and me as much as they were 1900 years ago. They are still there. They are still offered freely to all who are willing to have them. They are still the property of everyone who repents and believes. Let us glance briefly at them.

1. Set down, first and foremost, in your minds that there are unsearchable riches in *Christ's person*. That miraculous union of perfect Man and perfect God in our Lord Jesus Christ is a great mystery, no doubt, which we have no line to fathom. It is a high thing; and we cannot attain to it. But, mysterious as that union may be, it is a mine of comfort and consolation to all who can rightly regard it. Infinite power and infinite sympathy are met together and combined in our Saviour. If He had been only *Man* He could not have saved us. If He had been only *God* (I speak with reverence) He could not have been 'touched with the feeling of our infirmities', nor 'suffered Himself, being tempted' (Heb. 2.18; 4.15). As God, He is mighty to save; and as Man, He is exactly suited to be our Head, Representative, and Friend. Let those who never think deeply taunt us if they will, with squabbling about creeds and dogmatic theology. But let thoughtful Christians never be ashamed to believe and hold fast the neglected doctrine of the Incarnation, and the union of two natures in our Saviour. It is a rich and precious truth that our Lord Jesus Christ is both God and Man.

2. Next, there are unsearchable riches in *the work which Christ accomplished for us*, when He lived on earth, died, and rose again. Truly and indeed 'He finished the work which His Father gave Him to do' (John 17.4)—the work of *atonement* for sin, the work of *reconciliation*, the work of *redemption*, the work of *satisfaction*, the work of *substitution* as 'the just for the unjust'. It pleases some men, I know, to call these short phrases 'man-made theological terms, human dogmas', and the like. But they will find it hard to prove that each of these much-abused phrases does not honestly contain the substance of plain texts of Scripture; which, for convenience sake, like the word Trinity, divines have packed into a single word. And each phrase is very rich.

3. Next, there are unsearchable riches in *the offices which Christ at this moment fills*, as He lives for us at the right hand of God. He is at once our Mediator, our Advocate, our Priest, our Intercessor, our Shepherd, our Bishop, our Physician, our Captain, our King, our Master, our Head, our Forerunner, our Elder Brother, the Bridegroom of our souls. No doubt these offices are worthless to those who know nothing of vital religion. But to those who live the life of faith, and seek first the kingdom of God, each office is precious as gold.

4. Next, there are unsearchable riches in *the names and titles which are applied to Christ* in the Scriptures. Their number is very great, every careful Bible-reader knows, and I cannot of course pretend to do more than select a few of them. Think for a moment of such titles as the Lamb of God—the bread of life—the fountain of living waters—the light of the world—the door—the way—the vine—the rock—the corner-stone—the Christian's robe—the Christian's altar. Think of all these names, I say, and consider how much they contain. To the careless, worldly man they are mere words, and nothing more; but to the true Christian each title, if beaten out and developed, will be found to have within its bosom a wealth of blessed truth.

5. Lastly there are unsearchable riches in *the characteristic qualities, attributes, dispositions, and intentions of Christ's mind towards man*, as we find them revealed in the New Testament. In Him there are riches of mercy, love, and compassion for sinners—riches of power to cleanse, pardon, forgive, and to save to the uttermost—riches of willingness to receive all who come to Him repenting and believing—riches of ability to change by His Spirit the hardest hearts and worst characters—riches of tender patience to bear with the weakest believer—riches of strength to help His people to the end, notwithstanding every foe without and within—riches of sympathy for all who are cast down and bring their troubles to Him—and last but not least, riches of glory to reward, when He comes again to raise the dead and gather His people to be with Him in His kingdom. Who can estimate these riches? The children of this world may regard them with indifference, or turn away from them with disdain; but those who feel the value of their souls know better. They will say with one voice, 'There are no riches like those which are laid up in Christ for His people.'

For, best of all, these riches are *unsearchable*. They are a mine which, however long it may be worked, is never exhausted. They are a fountain which, however many draw its waters, never runs dry. The sun in heaven has been shining for thousands of years, and giving light, and life, and warmth, and fertility to the whole surface of the globe. There is not a tree or a flower in Europe, Asia, Africa, or America which is not a debtor to the sun. And still the sun shines on for generation after generation, and season after season, rising and setting with unbroken regularity, giving to all, taking from none, and to all ordinary eyes the same in light and heat that it was in the day of creation, the great common benefactor of mankind. Just so it is, if any illustration can approach the reality, just so it is with Christ. He is still 'the Sun of righteousness' to all mankind (Mal. 4.2). Millions have drawn from Him in days gone by, and looking to Him have lived with comfort, and with comfort died. Myriads at this moment are drawing from Him daily supplies of mercy, grace, peace, strength, and help, and find 'all fullness' dwelling in Him. And yet the half of the riches laid up in Him for mankind, I doubt not, is utterly unknown! Surely the apostle might well use that phrase 'the unsearchable riches of Christ'.

Let me now conclude with three words of practical application. For convenience sake I shall put them in the form of questions, and I invite each reader to examine them quietly and try to give them an answer.

(1) First, then, let me ask you *what you think of yourself?* What are your thoughts about yourself? Have you found out that grand foundation-truth that you are a sinner, a guilty sinner in the sight of God?

The cry for more education in this day is loud and incessant. Ignorance is universally deplored. But, you may depend, there is no ignorance so common and so mischievous as ignorance of ourselves. Yes: men may know all arts, and sciences, and languages, and political economy, and state-craft, and yet be miserably ignorant of their own hearts and their own state before God.

Be very sure that self-knowledge is the first step towards heaven. To know God's unspeakable perfection, and our own immense imperfection; to see our own unspeakable defectiveness and corruption is the A B C of saving religion. The more real inward light we have, the more humble and lowly-minded we shall be, and the more we shall understand the value of that despised thing, the Gospel of Christ. He that thinks worst of himself and his own doings is perhaps the best Christian before God. Well would it be for many if they would pray, night and day, this simple prayer: 'Lord, show me myself.'

(2) *Secondly, what do you think of the ministers of Christ?* Strange

as that question may seem, I verily believe that the kind of answer a
man would give to it, if he speaks honestly, is very often a fair test of
the state of his heart.

Observe, I am not asking what you think of an idle, worldly, inconsistent clergyman — a sleeping watchman and faithless shepherd.
No! I ask you what you think of the faithful minister of Christ, who
honestly exposes sin, and pricks your conscience. Mind how you
answer that question. Too many, nowadays, like only those ministers
who prophesy smooth things and let their sins alone, who flatter their
pride and amuse their intellectual taste, but who never sound an
alarm, and never tell them of a wrath to come. When Ahab saw
Elijah, he said, 'Hast thou found me, O mine enemy?' (1 Kings
21.20). When Micaiah was named to Ahab, he cried, 'I hate him
because he doth not prophesy good of me, but evil' (1 Kings 22.8).
Alas, there are many like Ahab in the nineteenth century! They like a
ministry which does not make them uncomfortable, and send them
home ill at ease. How is it with you? Oh, believe me, he is the best
friend who tells you the most truth! It is an evil sign in the church
when Christ's witnesses are silenced, or persecuted, and men hate
him who reproveth (Isa. 29.21). It was a solemn saying of the prophet
to Amaziah, 'Now I know that God hath determined to destroy thee,
because thou hast done this, and not hearkened to my counsel' (2
Chron. 25.16).

(3) Last of all, *what do you think of Christ Himself?* Is He great or
little in your eyes? Does He come first or second in your estimation? Is
He before or behind His church, His ministers, His sacraments, His
ordinances? Where is He in your heart and your mind's eye?

After all, this is the question of questions! Pardon, peace, rest of
conscience, hope in death, heaven itself — all hinge upon our answer.
To know Christ is life eternal. To be without Christ is to be without
God. 'He that hath the Son hath life; and he that hath not the Son of
God hath not life' (1 John 5.12). The friends of purely secular
education, the enthusiastic advocates of reform and progress, the
worshippers of reason, and intellect, and mind, and science, may say
what they please, and do all they can to mend the world. But they
will find their labour in vain if they do not make allowance for the
fall of man, if there is no place for Christ in their schemes. There is a
sore disease at the heart of mankind, which will baffle all their efforts, and defeat all their plans, and that disease is sin. Oh, that
people would only see and recognize the corruption of human
nature, and the uselessness of all efforts to improve man which are
not based on the remedial system of the Gospel! Yes, the plague of sin

is in the world, and no waters will ever heal that plague except those which flow from the fountain for all sin — a crucified Christ.

But, to wind up, where is boasting? As a great divine said on his death-bed, 'We are all of us only half awake.' The best Christian among us knows but little of his glorious Saviour, even after he had learned to believe. We see through a glass darkly. We do not realize the 'unsearchable riches' there are in Him. When we wake up after His likeness in another world, we shall be amazed that we knew Him so imperfectly, and loved Him so little. Let us seek to know Him better now, and live in closer communion with Him. So living, we shall feel no need of human priests and earthly confessionals. We shall feel, 'I have all and abound: I want nothing more. Christ dying for me on the cross — Christ ever interceding for me at God's right hand — Christ dwelling in my heart by faith — Christ soon coming again to gather me and all His people together to part no more, Christ is enough for me. Having Christ, I have "unsearchable riches".'

ANDREW MURRAY (1828-1917)

A Dutch Reformed minister in South Africa, Andrew Murray had spent seven years in Aberdeen, in his youth, to study for the ministry; and after graduating there he went on to Utrecht University, in Holland. Ordained at 20, he began his ministry at Bloemfontein. In 1860 he accepted a call to Worcester, an important town in Cape Colony. The (1859) Revival in America and Ireland reached his country and made a great impact upon his church. A pastorate in Cape Town followed (1864-71); then for 35 years he was minister of a Huguenot community at Wellington, about 45 miles from Cape Town. Described as 'the most influential leader of his own (Dutch Reformed) church of his generation', he was its Moderator six times. He travelled extensively, and was in great demand as a Convention speaker in America. During a further visit to England he spoke at the Keswick Convention in 1895, making a deep impression; and on his return home he started the South African 'Keswick', over which he presided until his death. He wrote numerous books of a semi-mystical nature, the most widely know of which, *Abide in Christ*, is still published in several languages; and from it the following chapter is taken.

THAT YOU MAY BEAR MUCH FRUIT

We all know what fruit is. The produce of the branch, by which men are refreshed and nourished. The fruit is not for the branch, but for those who come to carry it away. As soon as the fruit is ripe, the branch gives it off, to commence afresh its work of beneficence, and anew prepare its fruit for another season. A fruit-bearing tree lives not for itself, but wholly for those to whom its fruit brings refreshment and life. And so the branch exists only and entirely for the sake of the fruit. To make glad the heart of the husbandman is its object, its safety, and its glory.

Beautiful image of the believer abiding in Christ (John 15.5–8)! He not only grows in strength, the union with the Vine becoming ever surer and firmer, he also bears fruit, yea, much fruit. He has the power to offer that to others of which they can eat and live. Amid all who surround him he becomes like a tree of life, which they can taste, and be refreshed. He is in his circle a centre of life and of blessing, and that simply because he abides in Christ, and receives from Him the Spirit and the life of which he can impart to others. Learn thus, if thou wouldest bless others, to abide in Christ, and that if thou dost abide, thou shalt surely bless. As surely as the branch abiding in a fruitful vine bears fruit, so surely, yea, *much more surely*, will a soul abiding in Christ with His fullness of blessing be made a blessing.

The reason of this is easily understood. If Christ, the heavenly Vine, has taken the believer as a branch, then He has pledged Himself, in the very nature of things, to supply the sap and spirit and nourishment to make it bring forth fruit. 'From *me* is thy fruit found': these words derive new meaning from our parable. The soul need but have one care — to abide closely, fully, wholly. He will give the fruit. He works all that is needed to make the believer a blessing.

Abiding in Him, you receive of Him *His Spirit of love and compassion* towards sinners, making you desirous to seek their good. By nature the heart is full of selfishness. Even in the believer, his own salvation and happiness are often too much his only object. But abiding in Jesus, you come into contact with His infinite love; its fire begins to burn within your heart; you see the beauty of love; you learn to look upon loving and serving and saving your fellow-men as the highest privilege a disciple of Jesus can have. Abiding in Christ, your heart learns to feel the wretchedness of the sinner still in darkness, and the fearfulness of the dishonour done to your God. With Christ you begin to bear the burden of souls, the burden of sins not your own. As you are more closely united to Him, somewhat of that passion for souls which urged Him to Calvary begins to breathe within you, and you are ready to follow His footsteps, to forsake the heaven of your own happiness, and devote your life to win the souls Christ has taught you to love. The very spirit of the Vine is love; the spirit of love streams into the branch that abides in Him.

The desire to be a blessing is but the beginning. As you undertake to work, you speedily become conscious of your own weakness and the difficulties in your way. Souls are not saved at your bidding. You are ready to be discouraged, and to relax your effort. But abiding in Christ, you receive *new courage and strength for the work*. Believing what Christ teaches, that it is He who *through you* will give His blessing to the world, you understand that you are but the feeble instrument through which the hidden power of Christ does its work, that His strength may be perfected and made glorious in your weakness. It is a great step when the believer fully consents to his own weakness, and the abiding consciousness of it, and so works faithfully on, fully assured that his Lord *is working* through him. He rejoices that the excellence of the power is of God, and not of us. Realizing his oneness with his Lord, he considers no longer his own weakness, but counts on the power of Him of whose hidden working within he is assured. It is this secret assurance that gives a brightness to his look, and a gentle firmness to his tone, and a perseverance to all his efforts, which of themselves are great means of influencing those he is seeking to win. He goes forth in the spirit of one to whom victory is assured; for this is the victory that overcometh, even our faith. He no longer counts it humility to say that God cannot bless his unworthy efforts. He claims and expects a blessing, because it is not he, but Christ in him, that worketh.

The great secret of abiding in Christ is the deep conviction that we are nothing, and He is everything. As this is learnt it no longer seems strange to believe that our weakness need be no hindrance to His saving power. The believer who yields himself wholly up to Christ for service in the spirit of a simple, childlike trust, will assuredly bring forth much fruit. He will not fear even to claim his share in the wonderful promise: 'He that believeth on me, the works that I do shall he do also; and *greater works* than these shall he do, because I go to the Father.' He no longer thinks that he cannot have a blessing, and must be kept unfruitful, that he may be kept humble. He sees that the most heavily laden branches bow the lowest down. Abiding in Christ, he has yielded assent to the blessed agreement between the Vine and the branches, that of the fruit all the glory shall be to the Husbandman, the blessed Father.

Let us learn two lessons. If we are abiding in Jesus, let us begin to work. Let us first seek to influence those around us in daily life. Let us accept distinctly and joyfully our holy calling, that we are even now to live as the servants of the love of Jesus to our fellow-men. Our daily life must have for its object the making of an impression favourable to Jesus. When you look at the branch you see at once the likeness to the Vine. We must live so that somewhat of the holiness and the gentleness of Jesus may shine out in us. We must live to represent Him. As was the case with Him when on earth, the life must prepare the way for the teaching.

What the church and the world both need is this: men and women full of the Holy Ghost and of love, who, as the living embodiments of the grace and power of Christ, witness for Him, and for His power on behalf of those who believe in Him. Living so, with our hearts longing to have Jesus glorified in the soul He is seeking after, let us offer ourselves to Him for direct work. There is work in our own homes. There is work among the sick, the poor, and the outcast. There is work in a hundred different paths which the Spirit of Christ opens up through those who allow themselves to be led by Him. There is work perhaps for us in ways that have not yet been opened up by others. Abiding in Christ, let us work. Let us work, not like those who are content if they now follow the fashion, and take some share in religious work. No; let us work as those who are growing liker to Christ because they are abiding in Him, and who, like Him, count the work of winning souls to the Father the very joy and glory of heaven begun on earth.

And the second lesson is: If you work, abide in Christ. This is one of the blessings of work if done in the right spirit — it will deepen your union with your blessed Lord. It will discover your weakness, and throw you back on His strength. It will stir you to much prayer; and in prayer for others is the time when the soul, forgetful of itself, unconsciously grows deeper into Christ. It will make clearer to you the true nature of branch-life; its absolute dependence, and at the same time its glorious sufficiency — independent of all else, because dependent on Jesus. If you work, abide in Christ. There are temptations and dangers. Work for Christ has sometimes drawn away from Christ, and taken the place of fellowship with Him. Work can sometimes give a form of godliness without the power. As you work, abide in Christ. Let a living faith in Christ working in you be the secret spring of all your work; this will inspire at once humility and courage. Let the Holy Spirit of Jesus dwell in you as the Spirit of His tender compassion and His divine power. Abide in Christ, and offer every faculty of your nature freely and unreservedly to Him, to sanctify it for Himself. If Jesus Christ is really to work through us, it needs an entire consecration of ourselves to Him, daily renewed. But we understand now, just this is abiding in Him; just this it is that constitutes our highest privilege and happiness. To be a branch bearing fruit — nothing less, nothing more — be this our only joy.

CHARLES HADDON SPURGEON (1834-1892)

During the latter part of his life, Charles Haddon Spurgeon, the pre-eminent Baptist preacher, suffered frequent bouts of illness through gout; and he found relief and recuperation at Mentone, in the south of France. During these holidays it was his practice to hold private Communion Services in his drawing room, to which he invited friends and English-speaking visitors to the (then) secluded resort. A collection of the addresses he gave at these gatherings, with other Communion sermons, was published in 1894 under the title *Till He Come*. They possess the qualities which made Spurgeon's sermons so widely read in his own day, and ever since. The first of these addresses, delivered at Mentone but undated, is entitled 'Mysterious Visits', but we have changed this to the more explanatory 'Divine Visitations'.

DIVINE VISITATIONS

It is a theme for wonder that the glorious God should visit sinful man. 'What is man, that Thou are mindful of him? And the son of man, that Thou visitest him?' A divine visit is a joy to be treasured whenever we are favoured with it. David speaks of it with great solemnity in Psalm 17.3. The psalmist was not content barely to *speak* of it; but he wrote it down in plain terms, that it might be known throughout all generations: '*Thou hast visited me in the night.*' Beloved, if God has ever visited you, you also will marvel at it, will carry it in your memory, will speak of it to your friends, and will record it in your diary as one of the notable events of your life. Above all, you will speak of it to God Himself, and say with adoring gratitude, 'Thou hast visited me in the night'. It should be a solemn part of worship to remember and make known the condescension of the Lord, and say both in lowly prayer and in joyful psalm, 'Thou hast visited me'.

To you, beloved friends, I will speak of my own experience, nothing doubting that it is also yours. If our God has ever visited any of us personally by His Spirit, two results have attended the visit: it has been *sharply searching*, and it has been *sweetly solacing*.

When first of all the Lord draws nigh to the heart, the trembling soul perceives clearly the searching character of His visit. Remember how Job answered the Lord, 'I have heard of Thee by the hearing of the ear; but now mine eye seeth Thee, wherefore I abhor myself, and repent in dust and ashes.' We can read of God, and hear of God, and be little moved; but when we feel His presence it is another matter. I thought my house was good enough for kings; but when the King of kings came to it I saw that it was a hovel quite unfit for His abode. I had never known sin to be so 'exceeding sinful' if I had not known God to be so perfectly holy. I had never understood the depravity of my own nature if I had not known the holiness of God's nature. When we see Jesus we fall at His feet as dead; till then, we are alive with vainglorious life. If letters of light traced by a mysterious hand upon the wall caused the joints of Belshazzar's loins to be loosed, what awe overcomes our spirits when we see the Lord Himself! In the presence of so much light our spots and wrinkles are revealed, and we are utterly ashamed. We are like Daniel, who said, 'I was left alone, and saw this great vision, and there remained no strength in me: for my comeliness was turned in me into corruption.' It is when the Lord visits us that we see our nothingness, and ask, 'Lord, what is man?'

I remember well when God first visited me; and assuredly it was the night of nature, of ignorance, of sin. His visit had the same effect upon me that it had upon Saul of Tarsus when the Lord spake to him out of heaven. He brought me down from the high horse, and caused me to fall to the ground; by the brightness of the light of His Spirit He made me grope in conscious blindness; and in the brokenness of my heart I cried, 'Lord, what wilt Thou have me to do?' I felt that I had been rebelling against the Lord, kicking against the pricks, and doing evil even as I could; and my soul was filled with anguish at the discovery. Very searching was the glance of the eye of Jesus, for it revealed my sin, and caused me to go out and weep bitterly. As when the Lord visited Adam, and called him to stand naked before Him, so was I stripped of all my righteousness before the face of the Most High. Yet the visit ended not there; for as the Lord God clothed our first parents in coats of skins, so did He cover me with the righteousness of the great sacrifice, and He gave me songs in the night. It was night, but the visit was no dream: in fact, I there and then ceased to dream, and began to deal with the reality of things.

I think you will remember that when the Lord first visited you in the night, it was with you as with Peter when Jesus came to him. He had been toiling with his net all the night, and nothing came of it; but when the Lord Jesus came into his boat and bade him launch out into the deep, and let down his net for a draught, he caught such a great multitude of fishes that the boat began to sink. See! the boat goes down, down, till the water threatens to engulf it, and Peter, and the fish, and all. Then Peter fell down at Jesus' knees and cried, 'Depart from me; for I am a sinful man, O Lord!' The presence of Jesus was too much for him: his sense of unworthiness made him sink like his boat, and shrink away from the divine Lord.

I remember that sensation well; for I was half inclined to cry with the demoniac of Gadara, 'What have I to do with Thee, Jesus, Thou Son of God most high?' That first discovery of His injured love was overpowering; its very hopefulness increased my anguish, for then I saw that I had slain the Lord who had come to save me. I saw that mine was the hand which made the hammer fall, and drove the nails that fastened the Redeemer's hands and feet to the cruel tree.

> My conscience felt and owned the guilt,
>   And plunged me in despair;
> I saw my sins His blood had spilt,
>   And helped to nail Him there.

This is the sight which breeds repentance: 'They shall look upon Him whom they have pierced, and mourn for Him.' When the Lord visits us He humbles us, removes all hardness from our hearts, and leads us to the Saviour's feet.

When the Lord first visited us in the night, it was very much with us as with John when the Lord visited him in the isle that is called Patmos. He tells us, 'And when I saw Him, I fell at His feet as dead.' Yes, even when we begin to see that He has put away our sin and removed our guilt by His death, we feel as if we could never look up again, because we have been so cruel to our best Friend. It is no wonder if we then say, 'It is true that He has forgiven me; but I can never forgive myself. He makes me live, and I live in Him; but at the thought of His goodness I fall at His feet as dead. Boasting is dead, self is dead, and all desire for anything beyond my Lord is dead also.' Well does Cowper sing of —

> That dear hour, that brought me to His foot,
> And cut up all my follies by the root.

The process of destroying follies is more hopefully performed at Jesus' feet than anywhere else. Oh, that the Lord would come again to us as at the first, and like a consuming fire discover and destroy the dross which now alloys our gold! The word *visit* brings to us who travel the remembrance of the government officer who searches our baggage; thus does the Lord seek out our secret things. But it also reminds us of the visit to the physician, who not only finds out our maladies, but also removes them. Thus did the Lord Jesus visit us at the first.

Since those early days, I hope that you and I have had many visits from our Lord. Those first visits were, as I said, sharply searching; but the later ones have been *sweetly solacing*. Some of us have had them, especially in the night, when we have been compelled to count the sleepless hours. 'Heaven's gate opens when this world's is shut.' The night is still; everybody is away; work is done; care is forgotten: and then the Lord Himself draws near. Possibly there may be pain to be endured, the head may be aching and the heart may be throbbing; but if Jesus comes to visit us, our bed of languishing becomes a throne of glory. Though it is true 'He giveth His beloved sleep', yet at such times He gives them something better than sleep, namely, His own presence, and the fullness of joy which comes with it. By night upon our bed we have seen the unseen. I have tried sometimes not to sleep under an excess of joy, when the company of Christ has been sweetly mine.

'Thou hast visited me in the night.' Believe me, there are such things as personal visits from Jesus to His people. He has not left us utterly. Though He be not seen with the bodily eye by bush or brook, nor on the mount, nor by the sea, yet doth He come and go, observed only by the spirit, felt only by the heart. Still He standeth behind our wall; He showeth Himself through the lattices.

> Jesus, these eyes have never seen
>   That radiant form of Thine!
> The veil of sense hangs dark between
>   Thy blessed face and mine!
>
> I see Thee not, I hear Thee not,
>   Yet art Thou oft with me,
> And earth hath ne'er so dear a spot
>   As where I meet with Thee.
>
> Like some bright dream that comes unsought,
>   When slumbers o'er me roll,
> Thine image ever fills my thought,
>   And charms my ravished soul.
>
> Yet though I have not seen, and still
>   Must rest in faith alone;
> I love Thee, dearest Lord, and will,
>   Unseen, but not unknown.

Do you ask me to describe these manifestations of the Lord? It were hard to tell you in words: you must know them for yourselves. If you had never tasted sweetness, no man living could give you an idea of honey. Yet if the honey be there, you can 'taste and see'. To a man born blind, sight must be a thing past imagination; and to one who has never known the Lord, His visits are quite as much beyond conception.

For our Lord to visit us is something more than for us to have the assurance of our salvation, though that is very delightful, and none of us should rest satisfied unless we possess it. To know that Jesus loves me is one thing; but to be visited by Him in love is more.

Nor is it simply a close contemplation of Christ; for we can picture Him as exceedingly fair and majestic, and yet not have Him consciously near us. Delightful and instructive as it is to behold the likeness of Christ by meditation, yet the enjoyment of His actual presence is something more. I may wear my friend's portrait about my person, and yet may not be able to say, 'Thou hast visited me.'

It is the actual, though spiritual, coming of Christ which we so much desire. The Romish church says much about the *real* presence; meaning thereby the corporeal presence of the Lord Jesus. The priest who celebrates mass tells us that he believes in the *real* presence, but we reply, 'Nay, you believe in knowing Christ after the flesh, and in that sense the only real presence is in heaven; but we firmly believe in the real presence of Christ which is spiritual, and yet certain.' By spiritual we do not mean unreal; in fact, the spiritual takes the lead in real-ness to spiritual men. I believe in the true and real presence of Jesus with His people: such presence has been real to my spirit. Lord Jesus, Thou Thyself hast visited me. As surely as the Lord Jesus came really as to His flesh to Bethlehem and Calvary, so surely does He come really by His Spirit to His people in the hours of their communion with Him. We are as conscious of that presence as of our own existence.

When the Lord visits us in the night, what is the effect upon us? When hearts meet hearts in fellowship of love, communion brings first peace, then rest, and then joy of soul. I am speaking of no emotional excitement rising into fanatical rapture; but I speak of sober fact when I say that the Lord's great heart touches ours, and our heart rises into sympathy with Him.

First, we experience *peace*. All war is over, and a blessed peace is proclaimed; the peace of God keeps our heart and mind by Christ Jesus.

> Peace, perfect peace, in this dark world of sin?
> The blood of Jesus whispers peace within.
>
> Peace, perfect peace, with sorrows surging round?
> On Jesus' bosom nought but calm is found.

At such a time there is a delightful sense of *rest*; we have no ambitions, no desires. A divine serenity and security envelop us. We have no thought of foes, or fears, or afflictions, or doubts. There is a joyful laying aside of our own will. We *are* nothing, and we *will* nothing: Christ is everything, and His will is the pulse of our soul. We are perfectly content either to be ill or to be well, to be rich or to be poor, to be slandered or to be honoured, so that we may but abide in the love of Christ. Jesus fills the horizon of our being.

At such a time a flood of great *joy* will fill our minds. We shall half wish that the morning may never break again, for fear its light should banish the superior light of Christ's presence. We shall wish that we could glide away with our Beloved to the place where He feedeth among the lilies. We long to hear the voices of the white-robed armies, that we may follow their glorious Leader whither-soever He goeth. I am persuaded that there is no great actual distance between earth and heaven: the distance lies in our dull minds. When the Beloved visits us in the night He makes our chambers to be the vestibule of His palace-halls. Earth rises to heaven when heaven comes down to earth.

Now, beloved friends, you may be saying to yourselves, '*We* have not enjoyed such visits as these.' You may do so. If the Father loves you even as He loves His Son, then you are on visiting terms with Him. If then He has not called upon you, you will be wise to call on Him. Breathe a sigh to Him, and say —

> When wilt Thou come unto me, Lord?
> O come, my Lord most dear!
> Come near, come nearer, nearer still;
> I'm blest when Thou art near.

> When wilt Thou come unto me, Lord?
> I languish for the sight;
> Ten thousand suns when Thou art hid
> Are shades instead of light.

> When wilt Thou come unto me, Lord?
> Until Thou dost appear
> I count each moment for a day,
> Each minute for a year.

'As the hart panteth after the water-brooks, so panteth my soul after Thee, O God!' If you long for Him, He much more longs for you. Never was there a sinner that was half so eager for Christ as Christ is eager for the sinner; nor a saint one-tenth so anxious to behold his Lord as his Lord is to behold him. If thou art running to Christ, He is already near thee. If thou dost sigh for His presence, that sigh is the evidence that He is with thee. He is with thee now: therefore be calmly glad.

Go forth, beloved, and talk with Jesus on the beach, for He oft resorted to the sea-shore. Commune with Him amid the olive-groves so dear to Him in many a night of wrestling prayer. If ever there was a country in which men should see traces of Jesus, next to the Holy Land, this Riviera is the favoured spot. It is a land of vines, and figs, and olives, and palms: I have called it 'Thy land, O Immanuel'. While in this Mentone, I often fancy that I am looking out upon the Lake of Gennesaret, or walking at the foot of the Mount of Olives, or peering into the mysterious gloom of the Garden of Gethsemane. The narrow streets of the old town are such as Jesus traversed, these villages are such as He inhabited. Have your hearts right with Him, and He will visit you often, until every day you shall walk with God, as Enoch did, and so turn week-days into sabbaths, meals into sacraments, homes into temples, and earth into heaven. So be it with us! Amen.

ALEXANDER WHYTE (1836-1921)

Sometimes described as 'the last of the Puritans', Alexander Whyte was one of Scotland's most eminent preachers for over half a century—at a time when excellent preachers seemed to abound in that land. Born in Kurriemuir, and educated at Aberdeen and Edinburgh, he was minister of Free St George's, Edinburgh (1870–1909), where he had the largest congregation in Scotland. In 1909 he became Principal of New College, Edinburgh, and Professor of New Testament Literature. He was Moderator of the General Assembly of the Free Church of Scotland in 1898. A great preacher, writer and academic, he 'failed in no activity, but his pulpit was his throne'. Among his many books, the six volumes of *Bible Characters* are most widely known; also biographies of renowned 'worthies' of his own and earlier days. From *Jesus Christ our Lord*, his chapter on 'Jesus, Baptized and Praying' reveals his broad sympathies, particularly in his reference to the Salvation Army at a time when many churchmen eyed that movement with suspicion.

JESUS, BAPTIZED AND PRAYING

It is at the Jordan, says Luther, that our New Testament really begins. Our Lord, says the Reformer, was Jesus of Nazareth from His birth. But it was only at His baptism that He became the Christ of God, and it is only as He is the Christ of God that Jesus of Nazareth is really anything to us. All that is recorded about Him from His birth onwards is intensely interesting to us, and is indispensably essential to us. But that is so because the holy Child when He began to be about thirty years of age is openly proclaimed to be our Redeemer. His baptism is made the occasion of our Lord's ordination into His office as our Mediator; into His three offices as our Prophet, our Priest, and our King. And this was such an epoch in our salvation that the heaven opened and the whole Trinity, as the old writers used to say, came down to the Jordan that day. The Father came down and said, 'Thou art my beloved Son; in whom I am well pleased.' And the Holy Ghost descended in bodily shape like a dove upon Him. And, as for the second Person of the Godhead, that is He who is praying as He comes up out of the water. That is He who has been tabernacling among men now for thirty years, but who is today being publicly ordained to His ministry of reconciliation. Was Luther wrong when he said in his own bold, original and racy way that our New Testament really begins at the Jordan?

There is a very engaging and suggestive variety in the fourfold account we have of that great day's work at the Jordan. Matthew writes in his way, and Mark in his way, and Luke in his way. And while they are all at one in what they write, they are all so different in the way they write. And then John leaves the baptism out altogether, and in its place he gives us things that are of the intensest interest to us, and of the most supreme importance; and things, moreover, that we should never have known but for John's way of telling such things. John had so much still unwritten matter in his hands that, had he told us everything he had seen and heard, the world itself would not have contained all the books he could have written about his Master's saying and doings. 'But these are written that ye might believe that Jesus is the Christ, the Son of God; and that believing ye might have life through His name.'

'Suffer it to be so now,' said our Lord to the staggered and

protesting Baptist; 'for thus it becometh us to fulfil all righteousness.'
Now righteousness, you must know, is the sure foundation stone that
our Lord had come to lay in Zion. Righteousness is the first foundation stone of all our salvation. Righteousness, as a word, is the
greatest word for us in all our New Testament. And this is the first
time we come on this great word in all our New Testament. And then
it is a fine thing to see that the first occasion and occurrence of this
afterwards universal word is from His lips who is soon to be made the
righteousness of God to us. Our Saviour had been fulfilling all
manner of righteousness from His youth up; ceremonial righteousness and moral righteousness, legal righteousness and spiritual
righteousness: and He is but following out all that to the end when
He comes to the Jordan to be baptized by John. We are told that John
was perplexed beyond measure at the sight of our Lord presenting
Himself as a candidate for baptism among the crowds of penitent
people. But that was because John did not as yet aright understand
our Lord's motive in coming to be baptized. Our Lord did not come
confessing His own sins indeed; but He came to make Himself one
with them who did so come. You will sometimes see the saintliest
woman in all the city coming hand in hand with one of the
Magdalenes of the city, and taking her seat beside the chief of sinners
on the penitent form. That poor outcast would never have come to
that seat of salvation had not this Christ-like lady taken her by the
hand and led her in and sat down beside her; sat down beside her as
if there were no difference. Now if the General were to warn off all
such saintly women, he would be doing exactly what the Baptist said
and did at the Jordan that day. But our divinely-taught friend knows
better than to do that. So much better than that does he know, that
he sits down on the same form himself beside the offscouring of the
city. And thus it is that he gets his penitent form so well filled and his
Salvation Army so well recruited. It was something not very unlike
that when He who knew no sin came to the Jordan waters along with
the Roman soldiers and the Jewish publicans who were there confessing and forsaking their sins.

It is to the third Evangelist that we are indebted for this fine in-
formation that it was when Jesus was praying that the heaven was
opened (Luke 3.12). Our Lord prayed without ceasing, but there
were times and places when He prayed more earnestly, and His
baptism was one of these times and places. What all His thoughts
were as He descended under the water and came up again out of it is
far too deep for us to wade out into; at the best we can but adoringly
guess at His thoughts as He descended under the water and came

up again out of it that He might receive the Holy Ghost without measure so as to seal Him with all possible certitude to His great office, and to guide Him with all possible clearness as to how and when He was to enter on it. We can safely guess at His unrecorded prayer from the answer He immediately received to His prayer. For while He was yet speaking the heaven opened and the answer to His prayer came down. My brethren, will nothing teach you to pray? Will all His examples and all His promises, and all your own needs, and cares, and distresses, not teach you to pray? What hopeless depravity must there be in your heart when, with all He can do, God simply cannot get you to come to Him in prayer. 'It came to pass that, as He was praying in a certain place, when He ceased, one of His disciples said to Him, Lord, teach us to pray.' Will you not be like that disciple? Will you not tell your Saviour what a dislike, even to downright antipathy, you have at secret prayer; how little you attempt it, and how soon you are weary of it? Only pray, O you prayerless people of His, and the heaven will soon open to you also, and you will hear your Father's voice, and the Holy Ghost will descend like a dove upon you. Only pray, and your joy will soon be full.

The Holy Ghost had often descended upon our Lord's mother before He was born, and every day on Himself since He was born. At the same time this was a very special and an altogether extraordinary descent of the Holy Ghost at the Jordan. But why was it in a bodily shape like that winged creature which we call a dove? 'All apparitions,' says Thomas Goodwin, 'that God at any time made of Himself, were not so much made to show to men what God is in Himself, as to show how He is affected toward us, and to declare what effects He will work in us.' Excellently and enlighteningly said. For if there is one winged creature better fitted than another to symbolize how God is affected toward us, and what effects God would fain work in us, it is surely just a dove. 'For a dove, you know,' says the sometime President of Magdalen College, Oxford, 'is the most meek and the most innocent of all birds; without gall, without talons, having no fierceness in it, expressing nothing but love and friendship to its mate in all its carriages, and mourning over its mate in all distresses. And accordingly a dove was a most fit emblem of the Spirit that was poured out upon our Saviour when He was just about to enter on the work of our salvation. For as sweetly as doves do converse with doves, so may every sinner and Christ converse together.'

Quite so. And to go no further than His very first sermon, what could there be more dove-like than the text He took out of the evangelical prophet? 'The Spirit of the Lord is upon me, because He hath appointed me to preach the Gospel to the poor; He hath sent me to heal the broken-hearted, to preach deliverance to the captives, and the recovering of sight to the blind, to set at liberty them that are bruised.' Beautiful, is it not? Blessed to hear for the thousandth time, is it not? Remember the Jordan, then. Go often back to the Jordan. Look up at the opening heaven, and think that you see the descending dove. And at any time when you have to go to Christ again as a broken-hearted sinner, bruised and blinded with your sin, go back to Him thinking of the Jordan and of the dove, and pleading to yourself and to Him the argument of His favourite text. And then, in return to Him for all that, be you a very dove yourself. Be gentle, be kind, be helpful, be to all men a man of an approachable, affable, inviting, dove-like disposition. Be to all men a man after the manner of Christ to you, and after the manner of the dove among all the birds of the air. It is His own word to all His disciples: Be ye harmless as doves.

And a voice came from heaven which said, 'Thou art my beloved Son, in whom I am well pleased.' Think of it, my brethren. Never once since the fall of Adam and Eve had the Maker of men been able to say these words till He said them to Jesus Christ that day at the Jordan. Almighty God had often looked down from heaven to see if there were any that did good and sinned not. But when His eyelids tried the children of men it was always with the same result. Not one. Not Noah, not Abraham, not Jacob, not Joseph, not Moses, not David; no, not one single patriarch or prophet or psalmist or saint in all the house of Israel. But here at last is a man after God's own heart. Here at last is the second Adam, with whom God is well pleased. Listen well to these words, 'Well pleased'. Think with all your might who pronounces these words, and over whom they are pronounced.

Think, also, what all these words mean in His mouth who utters them, and in His ears and in His heart who hears them. And then, having thought all that well over, be entirely selfish for once. Turn to yourself and think what blessed words these words, 'well pleased', are for you. Think it out how these words bear on you, and how these words come all the way from the Jordan to belong to you. Think continually of what these words absolutely secure and seal down for ever to you. As, also, what they expect and claim of you. For one thing, these words, 'I am well pleased with my beloved Son', expect and demand that you shall as never before be very ill-pleased with yourself. These words, well pleased, rightly understood, and rightly laid to heart, will henceforth make every man who hears them to be more ill-pleased with himself than he ever is any more with anyone else. For then you will come to see that no one can give both God and man such constant cause to be ill-pleased with him as you can continually do. If you are ever satisfied with yourself, then Christ is nothing to you. He has come in vain so far as you are concerned. But if there is nothing and no one on the face of the whole earth who ever causes you so much pain and disappointment and dissatisfaction and displeasure as you continually cause yourself, then you are the very man to go straight to the Jordan, and to accompany Christ through all that baptism scene of His for you. Do not despair of yourself though you are far worse pleased with yourself than ever you were before. Do not despair of yourself so long as the Jordan runs in your New Testament.

Be as ill-pleased with yourself as you like, if all that only makes you better pleased than ever with Christ. It hath pleased the Father that in Him should all your fullness dwell. And if your displeasure, even to disgust at yourself and despair of yourself, only works round to make you of the same mind about His Son as the Father is, what more would you have out of this life of yours on earth? If you can look on Jesus the Christ coming up out of the water praying for Himself and for you as your Mediator, and if you will take home to your heart of hearts these glorious words spoken over Him by His Father, then His Father is well pleased with you henceforth, for His righteousness sake. And what more would you have? What more, what better, could God Himself do for you, or for any man, than to proclaim you accepted in His beloved Son. Beyond that even God cannot go. Beseech Him, then, to go that length with you and with me.

EVAN H. HOPKINS (1837-1918)

Born in 1837 in South America, Evan Henry Hopkins was the son of a civil engineer of Welsh extraction, whose work involved considerable travelling, so that the son was educated in South America, in England, and in Australia. He trained as a mining engineer, and was gaining an enviable reputation in that profession when he decided, at the age of 25, to prepare for ordination in the Church of England. After curacies in London's dockland and then at Portman Chapel — now St Paul's, Portman Square — he became the first vicar of Holy Trinity, Richmond, Surrey, in 1870. He was one of the pioneers of the Keswick Convention, and for 40 years was its most influential leader and speaker. He defined its teaching in his book, *The Law of Liberty in the Spiritual Life*, from which the chapter on 'Conformity to the Death of Christ' epitomizes the teaching of the Convention.

CONFORMITY TO THE DEATH OF CHRIST

What is the source of all practical holiness? It must have a source. Every river has a spring. In vital union with all fruit there must be a root. What then is the source of our fruitfulness? Not our renewed nature. 'That which is born of the Spirit is spirit' (John 3.6). Through the operation of God the Holy Spirit a spiritual nature has been imparted. But 'fruit' is not the outcome of our new nature, any more than in the vine fruit is the produce of the branch. The branch bears it, but the root produces it. It is 'the fruit of the Spirit'—the Holy Ghost. A bad tree cannot yield good fruit. Regeneration is essential in order that the fruit should be good. But the new nature is not the source. It is Christ Himself. There is only *one source* of all holy living; there is only *one holy life*. 'From me is thy fruit found' (Hos. 14.8). 'I am the life' not simply because I am the pattern of a perfect life, or because I am the bestower of the gift of life, but because I am the vital principle itself. He is the Spring itself. 'With Thee is the fountain of life' (Psa. 36.9).

It is Christ living within us. 'Not I', says the apostle, though I am redeemed. 'Not I', though I am regenerate, and have eternal life. 'I live; yet not I, but Christ liveth in me' (Gal. 2.20).

It was this that Christ promised. 'The water that I shall give him shall become *in him a well* of water springing up into everlasting life' (John 4.14). There is a progress in our apprehension of Christ as the life: a progress in our heart-knowledge of that fact. We see first the life in its source (John 1.4), then in its bestowal (John 3.16), then in its indwelling (John 4.14), and then in its practical outflow (John 7.38). It is in this last stage we have the 'fruit', the outcome of an indwelling Christ.

Here, then, is the source of all practical holiness. It is important to lay the emphasis on that word *liveth*. 'Christ *liveth* in me.'

What, then, is needed in order that this indwelling life should bring forth fruit abundantly unto God?

It is clear that divine life can need nothing from man to increase its vitality. It does not need our efforts to make it live. Think what it is we really possess, if Christ is in us. It was no mere figure of speech that the apostle employed when he declared that Christ was living in him. And what was true of him may be equally true of us. What, then, is it we possess? We have *Him*, in whom all fullness of life actually dwells, in whom infinite resources are stored up for our use. Everything needed for continual growth, for perpetual freshness, and for abundant fruitfulness is found in Him. All power, all grace, all purity, and all fullness, absolutely everything to make all grace abound towards us, in us, and through us, are stored up in Him who verily dwells within us.

Since this is so, what then is needed? Shall we try to help Christ live in us? Shall we try to make Christ more living? Shall we help Him to put forth His own power in us? Shall we try, in other words, to grow — to produce fruit? Surely not. And yet is not this the grand mistake multitudes are making? Something, however, has to be done. Something is needed to deepen our spiritual life. All Christians have Christ, and possess therefore all the resources of spiritual power and abundant fruitfulness; and yet all Christians are not abounding in fruit unto God. What is the reason for this?

It is here: though we cannot make Christ more living, though we cannot add to His infinite fullness of life and purity and power, we may be hindering the manifestation of that life.

One of the most serious hindrances is unbelief. This lies at the root of every other hindrance. But it may be urged that Christ has power to overcome this hindrance, and that He is able to break through this obstacle. And we know, of course, that He is able, that He could sweep away the barrier of all human unbelief. But is this the method of His working? Is it the law of His dealing with men?

We see Him entering a certain village. There were multitudes of poor and needy ones there. And He was ready to bless them. The sick and maimed were brought in crowds to His feet. But what do we read? 'And He did not many mighty works there *because of their unbelief*' (Matt. 13.58). Not that there was no manifestation of His power. 'He laid His hands upon a few sick folk and healed them.' But 'He could there do no *mighty* work' (Mark 6.5). His power was omnipotent, but it conditioned itself, as infinite power always does in the world; and by this limitation it was not lessened, but was glorified as moral and spiritual power.

But the incident throws light on many a passage in our own spiritual experience. The weakness and failure we have known arose, not from want of power in Him who has made us His dwelling-place, but from the lack of trust and confidence in Him, which He is ever demanding of us. We have limited the Holy One by our unbelief. We have 'set a mark' on the extent of His power to overcome and deliver, to keep and to save.

What then is wanted for the deepening of our spiritual life is the removal of every hindrance; and when we begin with unbelief, we lay the axe at the root of every other hindrance. But it is just here that the difficulty lies. It may be answered, 'By showing that it is a question of faith and not of effort, you do not remove the difficulty, you only shift it to another platform. How can I make myself more believing? I know it is because of my unbelief that I fail; but how am I to get more faith?'

This brings us to the main point. The truth is, we need *two* powers: a power to remove the hindrances, and a power to produce the fruit; a power to separate us from the evil, and a power to transform us into the good. This twofold power is found in Christ. There is the power of His death, and the power of His life. We do not bid good-bye to the first because we have been brought to live in the second. Nay, the condition of knowing the power of His resurrection lies in 'being made conformable unto His death' (Phil. 3.10).

The true life, that which triumphs over sin and 'does not cease from yielding fruit', is a life that springs up *out of death*. There is a deep spiritual meaning in those words of the apostle, which we fail to grasp at first sight, 'Always bearing about in the body the dying'—or the putting to death—'of the Lord Jesus, that the life also of Jesus might be made manifest in our body' (2 Cor. 4.10). Death is here put before us as the condition of life. The continual manifestation of the life depends upon the constant conformity to the death.

Death means separation, and life means union. By being brought more and more into sympathy with Christ's death unto sin, we become more and more thoroughly separated from its service and defilement. It is not merely separation from sinning; it is a separation from the old self-life. The great hindrance to the manifestation of the Christ-life is the presence and activity of the self-life. This needs to be terminated and set aside. Nothing but 'the putting to death of the Lord Jesus Christ' can accomplish this. Conformity to His death means a separation in heart and mind from the old source of activity and the motives and aims of the old life.

This 'conformity' is the condition of the manifestation of the divine life. As we have already observed, 'the life of Jesus' does not need our energy or our efforts to make it more living. All that God requires is that we should fall in with those conditions which are essential for the removal of the hindrances. Let those conditions be complied with, and at once the life springs forth spontaneously and without strain or effort. Though we can neither originate nor strengthen it by direct efforts of our own, we may indirectly increase its manifestation by complying with the divinely appointed conditions.

Our part consists in getting down into the death of Christ; His part is to live out His own life in us, just as the waters spring forth from the fountain. Then we shall know what the apostle meant when he said, 'Christ *liveth* in me'. Where Christ thus dwells in unhindered activity, there will be steady growth, perpetual freshness, and abundant fruitfulness; and the life will be marked by ease and spontaneity, because it will be natural.

From this we see that it is impossible to exaggerate the importance of understanding the meaning of His death. We must see that He not only died 'for sin' but 'unto sin'. In the first of these senses He died alone; we could not die with Him. He trod the winepress alone; as the sin offering He alone became the propitiation for our sins. But in the second we died *with* Him. We must know what it is to be brought into sympathy with Him in His death unto sin. Oneness with Christ in that sense is the means of becoming practically separated, not only from sinful desires, but also from the old self-life. And this assimilation to the dying Christ is not an isolated act, but a condition of mind ever to be maintained, and to go on deepening. 'Arm yourselves with the same mind: for he that hath suffered in the flesh hath ceased from sin' (1 Pet. 4.1).

Identification with the death of Christ is the great truth we learn in the Lord's supper. In the broken bread and the poured out wine, what have we but the symbols of His death? What is it that we especially dwell upon and make prominent in that sacrament? 'Ye do show forth His *death* till He come.' And by partaking of those elements we become identified with Him in that death. We become practically partakers of His life in proportion as we enter into His death, as we are made conformable in heart and mind to His death.

Wherever the blood of Christ is referred to in the Scripture, it means invariably His blood *shed*. The 'blood', we learn from the Old Testament (Lev. 17.10–11), is the life. 'For the life of the flesh is in the blood.' In consequence of possessing this character it could not be eaten; it was to be reserved 'to make an atonement for your souls upon the altar'. The clause, 'for it is the blood that maketh an atonement for the soul' may be more correctly rendered, 'for the blood maketh atonement by means of the soul', *i.e.* by means of the life which the blood contains. The blood is the vehicle of the animal's life; it represents that life. When it is shed—poured out—it represents that life as sacrificed: in other words, the *death* of the animal. The shed blood stands for the death of the victim.

Now when we speak of the 'blood of Christ', we mean the life

poured out, sacrificed; *i.e.* His *death*. There is a power in His death
to separate us from sin. All cleansing is separating; when a garment
is cleansed it is separated from that which defiled it. So the 'blood of
Christ cleanseth' — *i.e.*, the death of Christ separates — 'from every
sin'. The more thoroughly we are brought into oneness with that
death, the more fully shall we know what it is to be 'cleansed from all
unrighteousness'. . .

We now see that this 'putting to death of the Lord Jesus' — the
essence of His cross, if we may use the expression — is that which we
have to carry about within us always, as an abiding condition of
mind, since we need a constant and maintained separation from our
old self-life. This is not a matter effected once for all.

His death unto sin has therefore a most important and intimate
connection with our practical holiness. The condition of all real
progress will consist, therefore, in the being made conformable to
that death. Willingness to die to sin with Christ is a truer evidence of
the soul's advance than anxiety to be filled with His life . . .

The cross of Christ is therefore not only the place where we find
the new life, but also the place where we lose our old life. 'The
putting to death of the Lord Jesus' was the termination of that life
which is 'after the flesh', because 'our old man' — that is our old,
unconverted self — 'was crucified with Him'. To be brought into
oneness with that death, to be so identified with it that we, so to
speak, always carry it about, is to be walking in a condition of
continual deliverance from our self-life, and to find that the life of
Christ is being manifested in our daily walk.

All spiritual privileges are conditional. The condition of the 'life
abundant' lies in becoming a partaker of the mind of Him who died
unto sin, to be armed with that mind. This is not an isolated experience, a single act; it is a *mind* — that is, a spiritual condition to be
ever maintained, and becoming more and more deepened.

We have not therefore to strain our energies in order to live, or
increase our strength. The living Christ within us will put forth His
own power and manifest His own life; there shall be no lack of
vitality. But what we are required to do is voluntarily to submit to
die; and this, not by direct efforts upon ourselves, but by a par-
ticipation of the mind of Him who died unto sin once, and now lives
unto God.

The apprehension of the fact that we were identified with Christ
when He died on the cross unto sin, often produces most sudden and
decisive results in the experience and practical walk of the believer. It
cuts us away abruptly from our former course of life, and we find a

glorious emancipation from sin's power and service. But this effect, though sudden and immediate, is followed by a work which is progressive and continuous. Following the first apprehension of the believer's death with Christ, and its results, there is now a deepening work of assimilation of heart and mind to the crucified Christ, a more perfect bringing into sympathy with Him in His death unto sin.

And as oneness with the dying Christ becomes more and more an experimental reality, so the life increases — the living, risen Lord manifests His power, and fills the soul with His fullness. The believer's true life — that is, the life of Christ in him — is a life then that is ever springing up out of death. 'I die daily' is a declaration that is fraught with deep meaning, whatever may have been the sense in which the apostle used the words.

It is as we become practically identified with Christ in His death, that all the hindrances to the manifestation of His life are removed. In no other way can they be set aside. Our own efforts cannot accomplish it; our resolutions will utterly fail in effecting it, and leave us in despair. But God has provided us with a power by which every obstacle may be taken away. That power is the death of Christ. To get the benefit of that power we must submit to be conformed to that death, to be brought into actual sympathy with Him who died unto sin. Just as in the cross we find power which sets us free from the authority of darkness and translates us into the kingdom of God's dear Son, so in that death also we possess the power that separates us from the self-life and keeps us in a condition of deliverance.

Taking the 'blood of Christ' as equivalent to His death, and the effect of that death to be separation, we can understand how it is that the blood is continually cleansing us from every sin. Walking in the light, as He is in the light, the necessity of this constant separation from sin is felt more deeply continually. But the need is met by the divine provision, and we become more and more conscious of the power of that death to separate from sin of every kind; and hence the fellowship between the believer and God is maintained, and becomes a greater reality in his experience.

HANMER WILLIAM WEBB-PEPLOE
(1837-1923)

The son of a country parson who was also the squire of the parish, Hanmer William Webb-Peploe was a splendid athlete who at Cambridge represented his university at jumping and swimming. An accident in the gymnasium, however, kept him on his back for most of his last academic year, in which position he did his degree and ordination examinations. After a curacy and brief incumbency in Herefordshire, he became vicar of St Paul's Church, Onslow Square, London, in 1876, where he exercised a widely influential ministry until his retirement in 1919. He was a highly respected leader among Evangelicals in the Church of England, and a Prebendary of St Paul's Cathedral from 1893. Attending the very first Convention at Keswick in 1875 'as a visitor', he was called upon to speak and subsequently became one of its most trusted personalities for more than forty years. His addresses were delivered extemporaneously; standing with open Bible in hand, he would pour forth the Convention's teaching like a torrent, quoting Scripture prolifically from memory. In 1885 he delivered what is regarded as the most weighty utterance in all Keswick's history on the subject of 'Sin in the Believer', in answer to the teaching of 'sinless perfection' developed in some quarters and falsely attributed to Keswick. It is not a mere refutation of what he regarded as error, but also a penetrating presentation of Biblical truth.

SIN IN THE BELIEVER

I wish to put before you what I believe to be the mind of God on the subject of sin, in order that we may realize as believers in Christ what a marvellous blessedness it is for us to have the propitiation that God has given us in His own dear Son; for there seem to be many who do not quite understand what the Lord Jesus Christ has intended to do, or what it is that they really need Him for. They have accepted Christ for pardon; and they think that they have accepted Christ for one more final act of deliverance from all that can be called sin, when they offer themselves to Him for sanctification. All I would say at the outset is that if Jesus Christ gives deliverance from sin as a principle, as well as from sins committed, then that man must be living a more or less independent existence from the Lord. The Lord Jesus may be his Keeper; He may be his life; but He is not to him the Cleanser; He is not to him the Provider of perpetual acceptance in the eyes of God. Such a man is more or less compelled to live a life of personal self-satisfaction; he cannot centre his soul in Christ as a dependent sinner just from moment to moment.

The man who believes in a sanctification which eradicates sin from his person, as a principle, must be satisfied with his own condition, and be able to take his place more or less independent of the Saviour, even while he may say that he is dependent upon that Saviour for his vital joys and powers from moment to moment. My object is to trace what I believe to be the mind of God on the condition that attaches to man up to the last moment of his existence on earth—that is to say, however much Christians may have rejoiced in the Saviour, and have known experimentally the power of God the Holy Ghost; however advanced they may be in personal sanctification, they are, as I gather the truth from God's Word, dependent upon the grace of the Lord Jesus Christ for pardoning power, and for actual acceptance in the sight of God, to the very last instant they live upon earth.

If, by the power of God, we are enabled to see the actual personal condition of each man in regard to this terrible subject of sin, to the last, then, and then only, shall we apprehend what a glorious Saviour we have; what boundless tenderness and loving patience there is in the God of heaven toward His children on earth; what a boundless wealth of mercy there is in the Saviour, that He should continue to bear with the sinful condition of those for whom He died to make them God's true children for ever.

How is it that we are to write every man in this world down a sinner to the last moment of his life? You shall be judges of what God the Holy Ghost has set before us in the holy Word; and then if, by God's mercy, we come to a right conclusion of what is God's truth in this matter, there shall rest upon each of us the blessed privilege of just taking ourselves instant by instant to God as sinners to the last, saying 'God be merciful to me the sinner', and thanking God that there is not only a once-accomplished justification when I believed in the Lord Jesus Christ, but a perpetually-giving Christ for sanctification; so that without this perpetual action of Christ I should have to acknowledge myself at any moment to be lost, but that, thank God, I have to rejoice with a joy unspeakable and full of glory if I rightly accept the provision that God has made for me.

There appears to be a great anomaly—a regular paradox—in this statement that there can be this realization of sin every moment of a man's life; and yet that there can be an unspeakable joy and calm—for I adopt all that my beloved brethren have said before me with regard to the fullness of the liberty in Christ, and the provision made for us by that glorious Saviour. To say that a man must needs realize himself as a sinner at every moment, and yet walk in perfect liberty, in perfect peace, and unspeakable joy and security every moment in his life.

You ask, 'How can these things be?' Before I proceed to trace the mind of the Holy Ghost on sin, I ask you to realize the tremendously vital distinction between the penalty for sin committed and the guilt incurred at every sinful act, and the want of communion that may be realized when the soul is brought into a position of disturbance between itself and the great God in heaven.

I ask you to realize that at the very moment when you first believed in the Lord Jesus Christ as your Saviour, the question of the penalty for all sin, whatever it might be, and however much repeated in your daily life, has once for all been settled in God's sight independently of you altogether. You awake to it, and you clearly rest upon the finished fact from the very moment that you believe in the Lord Jesus Christ. The question of the penalty was settled at Calvary, and has nothing whatever to do with the sinner in regard to the provision God makes for him. The question of the penalty was between God and Christ. Christ satisfied the demand of the law, and granted in God's sight a complete pardon to all mankind who are willing to accept the provision by faith for all the sins they have committed; so that they are delivered at once by their faith from the penalty they have incurred.

But the question of the guilt being incurred is another thing altogether; and my affirmation that the child of God, however far he may be advanced, if he be enlightened by the Spirit, may awake to the consciousness that he has been incurring guilt in the sight of God, not because he has committed what are known among ourselves as definite acts of sin against the codes of morality and respectability that man puts forward, but because he has incurred guilt in the sight of God; because he comes short of the standard that God puts up, and it may be brought home to his soul that he has committed an act, or spoken a word, or thought a thought, from which guilt will arise in the sight of God. He should awake to the consciousness that every thought, word, and deed that proceed from him has, in a deep spiritual sense, brought guilt upon his soul by being short of the glory of God, lacking the perfect holiness of the standard that the Lord Jesus Christ accepted in His person.

But you will observe again, independent of the man, the provision that Christ Jesus made for sinners and for sin, keeps the man moment by moment cleansed from this guilt, altogether independent of his feelings or experience; that is the availing power of the blood, for though the man cannot walk in this mortal flesh up to the standard of the Lord Jesus Christ's perfection, and is therefore in that sense, and only in that sense, a sinner, yet he need never have a feeling of depression on account of these unconscious shortcomings, because the blood of the Lord Jesus Christ is cleansing him from all sin. That is the benefit of that glorious text. Moment by moment as the thing proceeds from the man, springing from the sinful nature that lies deep within him, unconscious it may be of guilt at the moment, yet incurring guilt, the man finds by the grace of God, that he is kept cleansed instant by instant, through the operation of the blood of the Lord Jesus Christ, in God's sight. That is the second great question we have to deal with: first the penalty, secondly the guilt.

Now, thirdly, the child of God is conscious of something altogether independent of the question of the penalty of sin and the question of his guilt. He is grieved at times — we have all found it so; he is disturbed in his blessed sense of communion with God by the fact that he has broken one of God's perfect enactments: he has come short of the glory of God; he has wandered in thought at least from God, and communion is disturbed. Now, the question of communion has to be settled, and communion can only be restored by an experimental action on your part. There is only one thing we can do as God's children: and what is that? If we confess our sins, He is faithful and just to forgive us our sins, and to cleanse us from all unrighteousness. So that when I awake to the fact of having in any sense broken God's holy law, I may instantly be restored to communion with my Father and my Saviour, and there is perfect peace in the soul again. We have a precious Advocate and a glorious propitiation in the presence of God; and therefore, if we discover our guilt and confess it, in that moment the restoration is complete. The blood has cleansed you, I believe, before you confessed, if you are a child of God; but the guilt requires to be taken away before you have perfect communion.

Keep short accounts with God; don't let your bills run up. If the devil entices you away from God, go to Christ at once and settle the guilt and have done with it. Bring your confession to God; and take it to the Lord, and in that very instant do trust God and believe that it is done away with. Don't go on burdening your soul with a sense of oppression. That is the devil's subterfuge, to keep you down when he can get you down by sin. He will keep you down by burdening your soul and blackening your life if he can. We have perfect salvation, and that is perfect communion. Keep clear by instantly confessing, directly you discover anything between yourself and your Father in heaven.

If you have followed me thus far, I am not afraid to trace out now what I believe to be the saddening condition that every man exists in to the last moment of his life on earth, and yet the glorious position we occupy in having such a perfect Saviour as God has made His Son Jesus Christ to be. The fact is that if there were no sin in a man on earth, I hardly know how he is to take up Jesus every moment and to sing His praises every moment; he would not need to do so, in my belief. He would not be conscious of a perpetual belief in the precious fullness even of the justification doctrine, and the sanctification provision made in Jesus Christ our Lord.

In Romans 5 we find, 'Where sin abounded, grace did much more abound; that as sin hath reigned unto death, even so might grace reign through righteousness unto eternal life by Jesus Christ our Lord.' Now I am not proposing to treat this subject in a general way, as a great announcement of the justification truth which is supposed to be the close of this great judicial passage of the Epistle to the Romans; but I take the words in verse 20 as their pure assertion, 'Where sin abounded, grace did much more abound'; and I want you to realize that sin abounds. Now, I believe that is contrary to many of our ideas. When we think of ourselves as pardoned sinners we fancy *sin* is put away as well as *sins*, and that from that moment we may begin to walk in perfect deliverance from any presence of evil. Are you prepared, as the Lord Jesus Christ has told us, to go to be judged? He is the kindest judge that ever lived; but He is also the most strict and stern that ever was known, and cannot abate one single jot or tittle of the law because you desire to escape from the exact standard that God puts before us.

When we speak of sin, you are perfectly aware that it is the inclination of the child of God as well as of the sinner to lower God's standard to suit our own condition. We read in some writings that sin is only what we consciously commit or say against the law of God or the requirements of our heavenly Father. Is that to be our standard? I say, God forbid that we should ever accept a standard with regard to the subject of sin which lowers God's requirements to our own possibilities, or to our own conception of what God really demands. Let us take the Word of God in all its fullness, and know sin as God has traced it before us.

Let us pass on to some of the passages from Scripture. In 1 John 3.4 we read these words, 'Sin is the transgression of the law.' Now, I suppose you do not admit as Christians that you have escaped from the law of God, or say that because you are saved you are not under the law, but under grace. The law is the expression of God's mind. The law of God is to be the delight of my soul. God has never changed the standard or altered the tone of the language. God has left the law what it always was—the actual expression of His mind and will; and therefore the law remains what it ever was. If you and I are under the Spirit, we bring forth fruit as far as God will enable us to bring it forth. In the first place, take the letter of the law and write that before your own souls, and ask whether you can say, 'All these things I have kept.' Thank God if you can say that you have kept the letter of the Ten Commandments. But what of the spirit of the law as Jesus enunciated it in Matthew 5–7—the look, the inward feeling of heart, these make adultery and murder; those feelings that the Lord Jesus has declared to be actually as guilty as an open act of the hand. What shall we say in regard to it? Thank God if you can say—though I doubt if your tongue would dare to say the words—'All these have I kept according to the Spirit.'

Go a step farther, and look at the tremendous expansion of the law. Go to Matthew 27.32 and onward, and with St Paul to Romans 13, on the doctrine of love—'Thou shalt love thy neighbour as thyself.' Will any man say he has kept that law? And once more, add to this the new law, the new commandment the Lord Jesus gives in John 13.34, 'A new commandment I give unto you, that ye love one another; as I have loved you, that ye also love one another.' Let us think of the meaning of that 'as', and then to hear a man say, 'I have kept that law' — 'love one another *as* I have loved you.' Let me ask you to realize that a transgression of the law is sin, and that if a man has failed for a single instant in loving me as Jesus loves me, that man is a sinner. We never loved each other as the Lord Jesus Christ loves us all.

Turn to a sentence in 1 John 5.17, 'All unrighteousness is sin.' According to the Greek the word means that everything that lacks the thoroughness and glory of the standard that God lifts up, is sin. What are we to say to this — everything coming short of the perfection of God is sin? 'The soul that sinneth, it shall die.' Go one step farther and look at the sins that may be committed by word. 'By thy words,' says our Lord in Matthew 12.37, 'thou shalt be justified, and by thy words shalt thou be condemned.' And in the preceding verse God says that 'every idle word that men shall speak, they shall give an account thereof in the day of judgment.' Now look at Proverbs 10.19, 'In the multitude of words there wanteth not sin.' God does not change His standard because that is Proverbs and the other Matthew; God's Word remains the same in Proverbs as in Matthew, and you and I must put Proverbs and Matthew together and have wisdom to see that in a multitude of words there is sure to be sin, and that for every idle word I shall be brought to an account with God.

I would go a step further, and ask, What about thoughts? Turn to 2 Corinthians 10.5. There we are told to 'bring into captivity every thought to the obedience of Christ'. Proverbs 24.9 tells us that 'the thought of foolishness is sin'; and remember that the soul that sinneth shall die. And that applies to God's saints exactly as much as to unsaved sinners, until we recognize the blessed truth I spoke of — perfect provision with regard to penalty, and perpetual provision with regard to guilt: that keeps the soul of man from perishing. Sinning is the same as being damned; so that we are perfectly right in saying that a child of God for one sin would pass to everlasting shame if it were not for the precious blood of the Lord Jesus Christ our Saviour.

Now with regard to other sins, we must take a general view of them. And what think you of such words as those in James 2.9, 'If ye have respect to persons, ye commit sin'? And what about those solemn words in James 4.17, 'Therefore to him that knoweth to do good, and doeth it not, to him it is sin'? Then such words as those in

Romans 14.23, 'Whatsoever is not of faith is sin.' And those words in James 3:2, 'For in many things we offend all.'

Every word of God testifies to one fact, that there is not a perfectly just man upon earth; that even when he is just, it cannot be said that he 'doeth good and sinneth not'. And why? Because Job, the most perfect man we read of, is brought into the realization of his true condition — of a man of whom it is affirmed 'that in all this he sinned not with his lips', yet when this man comes before God, with the perfection of God before him, he says, 'Behold, I am vile.' The man who would not let go his integrity, calls himself vile when he sees his God and recognizes his own condition. If that be the state of a holy servant of God, such as Isaiah, or Ezekiel, or Jeremiah, or Peter, or John, when he comes to the vision of the living God, when they see their inherent corruption, shall we not acknowledge that sin hath abounded? It is abounding and must abound as long as man remains with the inherent principle of evil indwelling their mortal flesh, and they are subjected to the lusts and corruption during the time that we are in a state of probation. I am convinced that it is good for us to be subjected to the presence of evil here; not to be under the power of evil — but its presence, whether it be physical disease or spiritual corruption.

Now many will ask, Why do I speak thus? Because I love the doctrines of grace, 'that where sin abounds, grace doth much more abound.' I mean by grace what I find in God's Word, and I have found that though it does not deliver me from the perpetual instigation and presence of evil and the principle of sin, the indwelling natural tendency and taste which once came from Adam, and which, as I believe, remains somewhere in the being of man to the last; yet I read in God's holy Word that while sin is always abounding, grace is infinitely more abounding.

It is a solemn thing to speak of grace much more abounding. There are parallel truths and parallel texts to meet every word that I have spoken on the subject of sin. There are parallel texts to all that I have uttered which proclaim that though God does not remove that indwelling principle or corrupt thing we call sin, yet He does by His infinite mercy give us a perfect, perpetual, and enjoyable deliverance from the activities, from the power, from the domination of sin, moment by moment, so long as we trust Him and acknowledge ourselves to be guilty sinners at every instant of our lives.

The doctrines of grace tell me that whatsoever sin hath done, Christ Jesus in His wondrous power hath more than undone with regard to the guilt and the penalty; it tells me that grace bringeth salvation. Look at Titus 2.11, 'The grace of God that bringeth salvation hath appeared to all men' — in the Revised Version it stands 'unto all men' — 'that denying ungodliness, we should live soberly, righteously, and godly in this present evil world.' Then, what is grace to bring me? That I read with regard to the Lord Jesus Christ in John 1.16, 'Of His fullness we have all received, and grace for grace.' Then in John 1.17, 'For the law was given by Moses, but grace and truth by Jesus Christ.' And in Romans 5.1-2, with regard to the grace wherein we should stand. Then go to Ephesians 1.7 and 2.7, where you will see references to the abundance of the riches of grace.

But more than this, what do I read about the daily provision for need up to the end of our lives? Turn to 2 Corinthians 9.8, 'And God is able to make all grace abound toward you; that ye, always having all sufficiency in all things, may abound to every good work.' What do I read in 2 Corinthians 12.9? 'My grace is sufficient for thee.'

A friend said to me, 'I thought you preached absolute deliverance from the principle of sin, eradication of the root of sin.' I said, 'God forbid.' 'Then,' she said, 'what is the difference?' My answer was, 'You preach a perfect sinner; I preach a perfect Saviour.' I thank God for a perfect Christ. Then, one said to me, 'If Christ was revealed to destroy the works of the devil, how can there be any sin left?' I replied, 'Dear brother, do wait a bit; Christ's day is coming.' The devil has had his day, and God's is coming. When God sees fit to take us away from this poor corrupt mortal flesh, corruption shall give place to glory, mortality to immortality, death to life and glory with God through all eternity. Saved by grace; kept by grace, when I ought to be condemned every moment for my folly; I shall be glorified by grace — and there shall be glory to God in the highest, and all through the realms of God's great universe, peace, joy, and gladness, for we shall be fully saved unto eternal glory when Christ comes. When we behold Him we shall be like Him, for we shall see Him as He is.

Oh, brethren, don't forget that while there is sin there is grace to meet all evil. O God, if this be true, make me to hate sin that gives Christ so much to do! Give me deliverance from all known sin. Reveal to me more and more what is the latent working and principle of sin. O God, open my eyes, show me more and more of Jesus. I will run the way of Thy commandments exactly so far as Thou in Thy mercy dost set my heart at liberty.

HANDLEY C. G. MOULE (1841-1920)

One of the few men almost invariably given the prefix 'the saintly . . .' like Fletcher of Madeley and Robert Murray McCheyne —
Handley Carr Glyn Moule was the youngest of eight sons of an
Anglican vicar. After a brilliant academic career at Cambridge, he
taught at Marlborough before his ordination in 1867, when he became curate to his father at Fordington, Dorset. In 1873 he returned
to Cambridge as junior dean of Trinity College; in 1881 he was
appointed the first Principal of Ridley Hall; and in 1899, Norrisian
Professor of Divinity. Marked out for elevation to the episcopate, he
succeeded Westcott at Durham in 1901. A convinced Evangelical, he
associated himself closely with the Keswick Convention. Of his
several books, *Outlines of Christian Doctrine* is still held in high
esteem; his expository volumes are invaluable; and from his
devotional books we have selected a chapter from *Thoughts on
Christian Sanctity*.

THE DIVINE MASTER

We turn our thoughts directly to the Lord Jesus Christ Himself, as the secret of all Christian holiness. The infinitely sacred subject can only be touched, and that only at a very few of its countless salient points. Intentionally I shall avoid many aspects, even paramount aspects, of the truth as it is in Jesus. I will but allude in passing to the Saviour as my Justification, my Sacrifice of peace, my Righteousness before a holy God. And I will but thus passingly allude to Him, for the present, as the great Firstborn among many brethren, the Second Man, the Root and Life-spring of the new race, of new men, of new man.

I would take just now these great underlying truths for granted. Let us come, carrying them always in the heart, to some of those holy phenomena of the surface, if I may so speak, which will be more immediately present to the consciousness of him who, in self-dedication and in simplicity of faith, steps out in an hourly walk with God.

First, I reverently place my Redeemer before me as my Master. This aspect of His sacred personality towards me comes thus first in the order of thought about Him, by no means at random. We think of Him as the Keeper, and as the Friend; and how many other titles might we not gather round His name, full of tenderness unspeakable! But if we would get aright at these, for use in the hourly path, for rest amid overwhelming pressure or inter-lacing cares, or for the spiritual mind amidst the common intercourse of common days, sure I am — deeply sure — that we need to lay beneath all these restful views of Christ, to weave as a thread of strength and truth into them all, the thought, the fact, that He is the Master, the Master of a veritable slave, and that slave here, now, always, everywhere, is myself.

True, there are texts in which the Lord and His apostles waive this idea for a special purpose. 'I call you not servants, but friends' (John 15.5); 'Thou art no more a servant, but a son' (Gal. 4.7). But a little attention shows that we have in such sentences, as often in Scripture, one side of truth isolated and spoken absolutely, while yet other sides hold good. He who calls His followers friends, says on the same occasion that they do well to call Him Lord. And soon He deals with them as Lord indeed: 'If I will that he tarry till I come, what is that to thee?' And the apostle who bids the believer repudiate in one respect the idea of bondage, clasps it in another to his inmost soul: 'Paul, the slave of Jesus Christ'; 'whose I am'; 'enslaved to God'.

Thus the idea is a permanent one, so permanent that it is carried on into the eternal state: 'His bond-servants shall serve Him, and they shall see His face.' And what I deeply feel and would earnestly enforce with regard to this idea, is that it is an idea precisely fit to give safety and solidity to every tenderer one. Fail to recognize it to the full, fail of an unreserved and habitual recognition that this is my despotic Master, a recognition carried into the inner habit of everyday thought and purpose, and there will be in every other aspect of Jesus Christ to me a something out of order, a lack of fixity, a lack of rest.

It is deeply significant that His own blessed invitation to the weary and the heavy laden, speaks at once of a yoke and a burden. How shall you find rest unto your souls? How shall you understand that I am meek and lowly of heart? Take my yoke upon you; become one of my 'servants under the yoke'. So, and not otherwise, you shall understand.

Let me look then every day and hour, and, as to the mental *habit*, every moment, upon Jesus Christ as my Master. Saintly George Herbert chose that to be, as it were, his best-beloved aspect of his Saviour: 'My Master, Jesus'; 'An oriental fragrancy, my Master' (*The Odour*). Let me do the same. Let me wear the word next the heart, next the will; nay, let it sink into the very springs of both, deeper every day.

Let me get up every morning with this for the instantaneous thought, that my Master wakes me. I wake, I rise, His property. Before I go out to plough or feed, or whatever it may be, upon His domain, let me with reverent and deep joy go into His private chamber, as it were, and avow Him as my Master, my Possessor; absolute, not constitutional; supremely entitled to order me about all day, and if He pleases, not to thank me at the close. Let me put the neck of self beneath His feet, and rise up bearing, not the cross only, which is another thought, but the yoke, the implement of menial service, the pledge of readiness to do and to carry anything. And let me continually, in the habit of my thought, be coming again into that Presence-chamber, to renew the act of that dedication and submission. With each call and claim the day may bring, let me carry into all things, let me have ready for them, this 'oriental fragrancy, my Master'. Is it regulated and expected duty? How delightful the thought that hands, or head, or voice, are indeed the implements of the faithful slave, kept at work for such an Owner! Is it unlooked-for and additional service? It is the Master's sudden call; I am wanted, and it is by Him. Let me rise with alacrity at His lightest bidding, and ask His pleasure. Is it the miscellaneous intercourse of life? Let my mental habit be so full of 'my Master' that I shall be on the watch, always and everywhere, to be used by Him, or to 'stand and wait' close to Him, as He pleases; only always knowing myself to be His property, and glad indeed so to be. Let others always know 'where to find me', as the phrase is; because I am bound and anchored to His blessed will by the realized and heart-welcomed fact of this thrice-holy, entire, and literal slavery.

Yes, and let me remember and welcome down into the depths of my being the fact that His despotism is above all things to be felt *there*. In my *innermost self* I have no personal rights against Him. Every thought is a lawful captive and slave to Him. No corner of that mysterious world, my spirit, no movement of will, or of desire, has a right to be other than He wills. I am bound, fast bound, to think as He does; to like and dislike with Him; to lay every personal prejudice and pique and so-called just sensibility on self's part beneath His despotic foot; and to leave it there, looking to Him to keep it down all day long. Let me never for one minute be content with the externals, however real in their sphere, of submission and of bondage. No; I am bound from within, from the depths. So it was of old when I lived that self-life I now deplore. The will was not free to righteousness; it was a slave-will, *that* way; and it was bound from within. Now it is not free to evil. It is a slave-will *that* way, and it is bound from within; for a Master, a despotic Possessor, dwells in my heart by faith. He says no. It is against orders. And the orders speak now in the region where to speak is to control.

So I take His yoke upon me, and I ask Him never to take it off; no, not for a minute. My gracious 'Master still bestows needful periods of repose'. He knows my frame. But when that repose does come, perhaps in some vigorous recreation in my youth, perhaps in calmer wise in maturer years, by shore or forest, on field or mountains, it is not for one moment release from slavery. The inner despotism is as merciful and as real as ever; and as to outward service, I am ever to stand ready for it. My Master has but sent me for renewal of strength to some fair corner of His domain, never off it; and will often meet me there, and remind me what I am, and may bid me work for Him there, if He sees it right. And He expects me to go back to the task when the rest is over, with all the blessedness of a renewed and absolute avowal of what I am, and for whom I live; 'an oriental fragrancy, my Master.'

And just the same it will be if He lays me low with sickness, accident, agony; bids me seemingly be useless for Him. Has He done it?
I am to ask no questions. Not for a moment am I a self-determining
being. 'Yes, Master; I know what I am, and I know Thee, and Thou
knowest me, and knowest best.'

Very feebly have I tried to sketch some practical, not sentimental,
exercises of thought and will upon those stern, those merciful words,
Master, Despot, Slave. May I dare to say they have become in
growing realization blessed realities to myself? Ah! how imperfectly
grasped yet; but enough to justify me, a sinner, in venturing to say,
'Taste and see that this Master, this unutterably real and despotic
Master, is good. There *is* rest here for the soul.'

It may seem strange to quote Aristotle in connection with
Christian sanctity. But there is a passage on slavery in the *Politics*, at
the opening, which I have lately read after many years with deep
interest and emotion. It is a ruthless statement of the principles of
bond-service of man to man, but we can read into it the golden gloss
of the bond-service of redeemed man to Jesus Christ. What is
Aristotle's account of 'nature's own slave', the being meant for
bondage? He is 'a chattel that lives'; he is 'a part of his master, as it
were a living, though separated, portion of his body.' He has, strictly
speaking, no existence apart from his master; he is 'not only the slave
of the master, but the master's, wholly his'; so that, in no action or
relation of life is he for one moment an independent being. On the
other hand — how finely and truly said! — there is thus and therefore
between the born master and the born slave a relation of common
interest and mutual friendship.

Are we not reminded, by the way, of that rule of the Passover
which entitled the born or purchased bond-servant to share the holy
meal with his master, but shut out the hired servant altogether?

Surely, in this page of Aristotle we find expressed to the letter,
almost to the spirit, the relation between the Christian and Christ.
The servant is the Master's piece of absolute property. He is a part of
his Master. He has no foothold for a moment's independence. He is,
as a 'slave by nature', by new nature, near to his Master, in closest
interest and in reverent friendship.

And further, still in Aristotle's words scarcely modified, 'he is by
nature a slave, as one made to belong to another, and as sharing in
that other's mind so far as to perceive it.' Yes, after all, the slave of
Christ, though purchased and branded for a most literal servitude, is
made capable of a true perception of his Master's mind; a sympathy,
as true as it is humble, with his Master's will; an intuition into his

Master's wish. And thus it is his delightful privilege evermore to act *as if* free, in just this respect, that he can look in his Master's face and say, as one who is at liberty to go if he will, 'I love Thee, I am well with Thee, I will not go out free.'

FREDERICK BROTHERTON MEYER
(1847–1929)

'A gentle, kindly, sensitive Christian gentleman' might well be the impression of F. B. Meyer lingering in the minds of those who knew him during the last decade of his life—as the writer of this brief memoir did. Born of a wealthy family of German extraction, he entered the Baptist ministry after graduating from London University, and held pastorates at Liverpool and York—where he helped the then unknown D. L. Moody to launch his evangelistic missions in Britain. In 1874 he moved to Leicester, and in 1881 resigned from the Baptist church there in order to establish Melbourne Hall as a centre of evangelistic and social welfare activity, in the same city. In 1888 he returned to London as minister of Regent's Park Church, and subsequently of Christ Church, Westminster Bridge Road. In both of these spheres he continued to battle against social evils, and to engage in welfare work, in a vigorous manner belying his 'gentle' appearance. He started a home for unmarried mothers, and an adoption society; and maintained his interest in released prisoners, for whom he had established a firewood cutting and selling business in Leicester. An inveterate globetrotter, he was a popular speaker at conventions in Britain and America, and a prolific writer—especially of devotional studies of Biblical characters, which still are widely read. His most treasured book, however, is *The Way into the Holiest*: Expositions of the Epistle to the Hebrews, and from it we take this chapter on Gethsemane.

GETHSEMANE

Eight ancient olive trees still mark the site of Gethsemane; not improbably they witnessed that memorable and mysterious scene referred to in Hebrews 5.7–8. And what a scene was that! It had stood alone in unique and unapproachable wonder, had it not been followed by 15 hours of even greater mystery.

The strongest words in Greek language are used to tell of the keen anguish through which the Saviour passed within those garden walls. 'He *began* to be sorrowful'; as if in all His past experiences He had never known what sorrow was! 'He was sore amazed'; as if His mind were almost dazed and overwhelmed. 'He was very heavy', His spirit stooped beneath the weight of His sorrows, as afterwards His body stooped beneath the weight of His cross; or the word may mean that He was so distracted with sorrow as to be almost beside Himself. And the Lord Himself could not have found a stronger word than He used when He said, 'My soul is exceeding sorrowful, even unto death.'

But the evangelist Luke gives us the most convincing proof of His anguish when he tells us that His sweat, like great beads of blood, fell upon the ground, touched by the slight frost, and in the cold night air. The finishing touch is given in the words which tell of His 'strong crying and tears' (Heb. 5.7).

THE THINGS WHICH HE SUFFERED. What were they? *They were not those of the Substitute*. The tenor of Scripture goes to show that the work of substitution was really wrought out upon the cross. There, the robe of our completed righteousness was woven from the top throughout. It was on the *tree* that He bare our sins in His own body. It was by His *blood* that He brought us nigh to God. It was by the *death* of God's Son that we have been reconciled to God; and the repeated references of Scripture to sacrifice, indicate that in the act of dying *that* was done which magnifies the law and makes it honourable, and removes every obstacle that had otherwise prevented the love of God from following out its purpose of mercy.

We shall never fully understand here how the Lord Jesus made reconciliation for the sins of the world, or how that which He bore could be an equivalent for the penalty due from a sinful race. We have no standard of comparison; we have no line long enough to let us down into the depths of that unexplored mystery; but we may

thankfully accept it as a fact stated on the page of Scripture per-
petually, that He did that which put away the curse, atoned for
human guilt, and was more than equivalent to all those sufferings
which a race of sinful men must otherwise have borne. The mystery
defies our language, but it is apprehended by faith; and as she stands
upon her highest pinnacles, love discerns the meaning of the death of
Christ by a spiritual instinct, though as yet she has not perfectly
learnt the language in which to express her conception of the
mysteries that circle around the cross. It may be that in thousands of
unselfish actions she is acquiring the terms in which some day she will
be able to understand and explain it all.

But all that we need insist on here is that the sufferings of the
garden are not to be included in the act of substitution, though they
were closely associated with it. Gethsemane was not the altar, but the
way to it.

*Our Lord's suffering in Gethsemane could hardly arise from the
fear of His approaching physical sufferings.* Such a supposition seems
wholly inconsistent with the heroic fortitude, the majestic silence, the
calm ascendancy over suffering with which He bore Himself till He
breathed out His spirit, and which drew from a hardened and
worldly Roman expressions of respect.

Besides, if the mere prospect of scourging and crucifixion drew
from our Lord these strong crying and tears and bloody sweat, He
would surely stand on a lower level than that to which multitudes of
His followers attained through faith in Him. Old men like Polycarp,
tender maidens like Blandina, timid boys like Attalus, have contemplated beforehand with unruffled composure, and have endured
with unshrinking fortitude deaths far more awful, more prolonged,
more agonizing. Degraded criminals have climbed the scaffold
without a tremor or a sob; and surely the most exalted faith ought to
bear itself as bravely as the most brutal indifference in the presence
of the solemnities of death and eternity. It has been truly said that
there is no passion in the mind of man, however weak, which cannot
master the fear of death; and it is therefore impossible to suppose
that the fear of physical suffering and disgrace could have so shaken
our Saviour's spirit.

*But He anticipated the suffering that He was to endure as the
propitiation for sin.* He knew that He was about to be brought into
the closest association with the sin which was devastating human
happiness and grieving the divine nature. He knew, since He had so
identified Himself with our fallen race, that in a very deep and
wonderful way He was to be made sin and to bear our curse and

shame, cast out by man, and apparently forsaken by God. He knew, as we shall never know, the exceeding sinfulness and horror of sin; and what it was to be the meeting-place where the iniquities of our race should converge, to become the scapegoat charged with guilt not His own, to bear away the sins of the world. All this was beyond measure terrible to one so holy and sensitive as He.

He had long foreseen it. He was the Lamb slain from before the foundation of the world. Each time a lamb was slain by a conscience-stricken sinner, or a scapegoat let go into the wilderness, or a pigeon dipped into flowing water encrimsoned by the blood of its mate, He had been reminded of what was to be. He knew before His incarnation where in the forest the seedling was growing to a sapling from the wood of which His cross would be made. He even nourished it with His rain and sun. Often during His public ministry He was evidently looking beyond the events that were transpiring around Him to that supreme event which He called 'His hour'. And as it came nearer, His human soul was overwhelmed at the prospect of having to sustain the weight of a world's sin. His human nature did not shrink from death as death; but from the death which He was to die as the propitiation for our sins, and not for ours only, but for those of the whole world.

Six months before His death He had set His face to go to Jerusalem, with such a look of anguish upon it as to fill the hearts of His disciples with consternation. When the questions of the Greeks reminded Him that He must shortly fall into the ground and die, His soul became so troubled that He cried, 'Father, save me from this hour!' And now, with strong cryings and tears, He made supplication to His Father, asking that if it were possible the cup might pass from Him. In this His human soul spoke. As to His divinely-wrought purpose of redemption, there was no vacillation or hesitation. But, as man, He asked whether there might not be another way of accomplishing the redemption on which He had set His heart.

But there was no other way. The Father's will, which He had come down from heaven to do, pointed along the rugged, flinty road that climbed Calvary and passed over it down to the grave. And at once He accepted His destiny, and with the words, 'If this cup may not pass from me, except I drink it, Thy will be done' He stepped forth on the flints that were to cut those blessed feet, drawing from them streams of blood.

HIS STRONG CRYING AND TEARS. Our Lord betook Himself to that resource which is within the reach of all, and which is peculiarly precious to those who are suffering and tempted—He prayed. His heart was overwhelmed within Him; and He poured out all His anguish into His Father's ears, with strong crying and tears. Let us note the characteristics of that prayer, that we, too, may be able to pass through our dark hours when they come.

It was *secret* prayer. Leaving the majority of His disciples at the garden gate, He took with Him the three who had stood beside Jairus's dead child, and had beheld the radiance that steeped Him in His transfiguration. They alone might see Him tread the winepress: but even they were left at a stone's cast, whilst He went forward alone into the deeper shadow. We are told that they became overpowered with sleep; so that no mortal ear heard the whole burden of that marvellous prayer, some fitful snatches of which are preserved in the Gospels.

It was *humble* prayer. The evangelist Luke says that He knelt. Another says that He fell on His face. Being formed in fashion as a man, He humbled Himself and became obedient to death, even the death of the cross. And it may be that even then He began to recite that marvellous psalm which was so much on His lips during the last hours, saying, 'I am a worm, and no man; a reproach of men and despised of the people.'

It was a *filial* prayer. Matthew describes our Lord as saying, 'O my Father'; and Mark tells us He used the endearing term which was often spoken by the prattling lips of little Jewish children, *Abba*. For the most part, He probably spoke Greek; but Aramaic was the language of His childhood, the language of the dear home in Nazareth. In the hour of mortal agony, the mind ever reverts to the associations of its first awakening. The Saviour, therefore, appearing to feel that the more stately Greek did not sufficiently express the deep yearnings of His heart, substituted for it the more tender language of earlier years. Not 'Father' only, but 'Abba, Father'.

It was *earnest* prayer. 'He prayed more earnestly', and one proof of this appears in this repetition of the same words. It was as if His nature were too oppressed to be able to express itself in a variety of phrase, such as might indicate a certain leisure and liberty of thought. One strong current of anguish running at its highest could only strike one monotone of grief, like the note of the storm or the flood. Back, and back again, came the words, '*cup* . . . *pass* . . . *will* . . . *Father*.' And the sweat of blood, pressed from His forehead, as the red juice of the grape beneath the heavy foot of the peasant, witnessed to the intensity of His soul.

It was *submissive* prayer. Matthew and Mark quote this sentence, 'Nevertheless not what I will, but what Thou wilt.' Luke quotes this,

'Father, If Thou be willing, remove this cup from me; nevertheless, not my will, but Thine be done.'

Jesus was the Father's Fellow—co-equal in His divine nature; but for the purpose of redemption it was needful that He should temporarily divest Himself of the use of the attributes of His deity, and live a truly human life. As man He carefully marked each symptom of His Father's will, from the day when it prompted Him to linger behind His parents in the temple; and He always instantly fulfilled His behests. 'I came down from heaven,' He said, 'not to do mine own will, but the will of Him that sent me.' This was the yoke He bore, and in taking it, He found rest unto His soul. Whatever was the danger or difficulty into which such obedience might carry Him, He ever followed the beacon-cloud of the divine will, sure that the manna of daily strength would fall, and that the deep, sweet waters of peace would follow where it led the way. That way now seemed to lead through the heart of a fiery furnace. There was no alternative than to follow; and He elected to do so, nay, was glad even then, with a joy that the cold waters of death could not extinguish. At the same time He learnt what obedience meant, and gave an example of it that shone out with unequalled majesty, purity, and beauty, unparalleled in the annals of the universe. As man, our Lord then learnt how much was meant by that word *obedience*. 'He learnt obedience.' And now He asks that we should obey Him, as He obeyed God. 'Unto them that *obey* Him.'

Sometimes the path of the Christian's obedience becomes very difficult. It climbs upwards; the gradient is continually steeper, the foothold ever more difficult; and, as the evening comes, the nimble climber of the morning creeps slowly forward on hands and knees. The day is never greater than the strength; but as the strength grows by use, the demands upon it are greater, and the hours longer. At last a moment may come when we are called for God's sake to leave some dear circle; to risk the loss of name and fame; to relinquish the cherished ambition of a life; to incur obloquy, suffering, and death; to drink the bitter cup; to enter the brooding cloud; to climb the smoking mount. Ah! then we too learn what obedience means; and we have no resource but in strong cryings and tears.

In such hours pour out thy heart in audible cries. Plentifully mingle the name 'Father' with thine entreaties. Fear not to repeat the same words. Look not to man; he cannot understand thee: but to Him who is nearer to thee than thy dearest. So shalt thou get calmer and quieter, until thou rest in His will; as a child, worn out by a tempest of passion, sobs itself to sleep in its mother's breast.

THE ANSWER. 'He was heard for His godly fear.' His holy reference and devotion to His Father's will made it impossible that His prayers should be unanswered: although, as it so often happens, the answer came in another way than His fears had suggested. The cup was not taken away, but the answer came. It came in the mission of the angel that stood beside Him. It came in the calm serenity with which He met the brutal crowd that soon filled that quiet garden with their coarse voices and trampling feet. It came in His triumph over the grave. It came in His being perfected as mediator, to become unto all them that obey Him the author of eternal salvation, and a High Priest for ever after the order of Melchizedek.

Prayers prompted by love and in harmony with godly fear are never lost. We may ask for things which it would be unwise and unkind of God to grant; but in that case His goodness shows itself rather in the refusal than in the assent. And yet the prayer is heard and answered. Strength is instilled into the fainting heart. The faithful and merciful High Priest does for us what the angel essayed to do for Him; but how much better, since He has learnt so much of the art of comfort in the school of suffering! And out of it the way finally emerges into life, though we have left the right hand and foot in the grave behind us. We also discover that we have learnt the art of becoming channels of eternal salvation to those around us. Ever since Jesus suffered there, Gethsemane has been threaded by the King's highway that passes through it to the New Jerusalem. And in its precincts God has kept many of His children, to learn obedience by the things that they suffer, and to learn the divine art of comforting others as they themselves have been comforted by God.

There are comparatively few to whom Jesus does not say, at some time in their lives, 'Come and watch with me'. He takes us with Him into the darksome shadows of the winepress, though there are recesses of shade, at a stone's cast, where He must go alone. Let us not misuse the precious hours in the heavy slumbers of insensibility. There are lessons to be learnt there which can be acquired nowhere else; but if we heed not His summons to watch with Him, it may be that He will close the precious opportunity by bidding us sleep on and take our rest, because the allotted term has passed, and the hour of a new epoch has struck. If we fail to use for prayer and preparation the sacred hour that comes laden with opportunities for either; if we sleep instead of watching with our Lord: what hope have we of being able to play a noble part when the flashing lights and the trampling feet announce the traitor's advent? Squander the moments of preparation, and you have to rue their loss through all the coming years!

JAMES STALKER (1848-1927)

Splendidly sustaining the Scottish tradition of scholarly preacher-writers, James Stalker was born in Crieff and educated at Edinburgh, Berlin and Halle Universities. He was minister of United Free Church parishes in Kirkcaldy and Glasgow before becoming Professor of Church History in the UF College at Aberdeen in 1902. A humble-minded man, he declined both a Principalship and the Moderatorial Chair of his church. He paid frequent visits to America, as visiting lecturer at colleges and seminaries; and was one of the eminent Scottish ministers who supported the Moody and Sankey missions in Scotland. His most widely known books are his 'lives' of Jesus Christ and of St Paul, *Imago Christi*, and *The Two St. Johns*, but our selection is a chapter from *The Trial and Death of Jesus Christ*, which has had a profound effect upon the thought and devotional life of the compiler of this volume from his student days.

THE SIXTH WORD FROM THE CROSS

Like the fifth, the sixth word from the cross, 'It is finished', is in the Greek literally a single word; and it has been often affirmed to be the greatest single word ever uttered. It may be said to comprehend in itself the salvation of the world; and thousands of human souls, in the agony of conviction or in the crisis of death, have laid hold of it as the drowning sailor grasps the lifebuoy.

Sometimes it has been interpreted as merely the last sign of ebbing life; as if the meaning were, It is all over; this long agony of pain and weakness is done at last. But the dying words of Jesus were not spoken in that tone. The fifth word, we are expressly told, was uttered with a loud voice; so was the seventh; and although this is not expressly stated about the sixth, the likelihood is that, in this respect, it resembled the other two. It was not a cry of defeat, but of victory.

Both the suffering of our Lord and His work were finishing together; and it is natural to suppose that He was referring to both. Suffering and work are the two sides of every life, the one predominating in some cases, and the other in others. In the experience of Jesus both were prominent: He had both a great work to accomplish, and He suffered greatly in the process of achieving it. But now both have been brought to a successful close; and this is what the sixth word expresses. It is therefore, first, the *Worker's Cry of Achievement*; and, secondly, the *Sufferer's Cry of Relief*.

I

Christ, when on earth, had a great work on hand, which was now finished.

The dying word carries us back to the first word from His lips which has been preserved to us: 'Wist ye not that I must be about my Father's business?' Even at twelve years of age He already knew that there was a business entrusted to Him by His Father in heaven, about which His thoughts had to be occupied. We cannot perhaps say that then already He comprehended it in its whole extent. It was to grow upon Him with the development of His manhood. In lonely meditations in the fields and pastures of Nazareth it seized and inspired His mind. As He cultivated the life of prayer it became more and more His settled purpose. The more He became acquainted with human nature, and with the character and the needs of His own age, the more clearly did it rise before Him. As He heard and read the Scriptures of the Old Testament, He saw it hinted and foreshadowed in type and symbol, in rite and institution, in law and prophets. There He found the programme of His life sketched out beforehand; and perhaps one of His uppermost thoughts when He said, 'It is finished', was that all which had been foretold about Him in the ancient Scriptures had been fulfilled.

After His public life commenced, the sense of being charged with a task which He had to fulfil was one of the master-thoughts of His life. It was written on His very face and bodily gait. He never had the easy, indeterminate air of one who does not know what he means to do in the world. 'I have a baptism', He would say, 'to be baptized with, and how am I straitened till it be accomplished.' In a rapt moment, at the well of Sychar, after His interview with the Samaritan woman, when His disciples proffered Him food, He put it away from Him, saying, 'I have meat to eat that ye know not of', and He added, 'My meat is to do the will of Him that sent me, and to finish His work.' On His last journey to Jerusalem, as He went on in front of His disciples, they were amazed, and as they followed they were afraid. His purpose possessed Him; He was wholly in it, body, soul and spirit. He bestowed on it every scrap of power He possessed, and every moment of His time. Looking back now from the close of life, He has not to regret that any talent has been either abused or left unused. All have been husbanded for the one purpose, and all lavished on the work.

What was this work of Christ? In what terms shall we express it? At all events it was a greater work than any other son of man has ever attempted. Men have attempted much, and some of them have given themselves to their chosen enterprises with extraordinary devotion and tenacity. The conqueror has devoted himself to his scheme of subduing the world; the patriot to the liberation of his country; the philosopher to the enlargement of the realm of knowledge; the inventor has rummaged with tireless industry among the secrets of nature; and the discoverer has risked his life in opening up untrodden continents, and died with his face to his task. But none ever undertook a task worthy to be compared with that which engrossed the mind of Jesus.

It was a work for God with men, and it was a work for men with God.

The thought that it was a work for God, with which God had

charged Him, was often in Christ's mouth, and this consciousness was one of the chief sources of His inspiration. 'I must work the work of Him that sent me while it is day', He would say; or, 'Therefore doth my Father love me, because I do always those things which please Him'. And at the close of His life-work He said, in words closely related to those of our text, 'I have glorified Thee on the earth, I have finished the work which Thou gavest me to do.' This was His task, to glorify God on the earth — to make known the Father to the children of men.

But just as obviously it was a work for men with God. This was stamped on all His words and on the entire tenor of His life. He was bringing men back to God, and He had to remove the obstacles which stood in the way. He had to roll away the stone from the sepulchre in which humanity was entombed, and call the dead to come forth. He had to press His weight against the huge iron gates of human guilt and doom, and force them open. He had done so; and as He said 'It is finished', He was at the same time saying to all mankind, 'Behold, I have set before you an open door, and no man can shut it.'

The more difficult and prolonged any task is, the greater is the satisfaction of finishing it. Everyone knows what it is, after accomplishing anything on which a great deal of labour has been bestowed, or the accomplishment of which has been delayed, to be able to say, 'There, it is finished at last.' In the more signal efforts of human genius and energy there is a satisfaction of final achievement which warms even spectators with sympathy at the distance of hundreds of years. What must it be to the poet, after equipping himself by the labours of a lifetime with the stores of knowledge and the skill in the use of language requisite for the composition of a 'Divine Comedy', or a 'Paradise Lost', and after wearing himself lean for many years at his task, to be able at last, when the final line has been penned, to write *Finis* at the bottom of his performance? What must it have been to Columbus, after he had worn his life out in seeking the patronage necessary for his undertaking, and endured the perils of voyaging in stormy seas and among mutinous mariners, to see at last the sunlight on the peaks of Darien, which informed him that his dream was true and his life-work accomplished? When we read how William Wilberforce, the champion of slave emancipation, heard on his deathbed, a few hours before he breathed his last, that the British Legislature had agreed to the expenditure necessary to secure the object to which he had sacrificed his life, what heart can refuse its tribute of sympathetic joy as it thinks of him expiring with the shouts of emancipated millions in his ears? These are feeble suggestions of the triumph with which Christ saw, fallen behind Him, His accomplished task, as He cried, 'It is finished'.

II

If Jesus had during life a vast work on hand which He was able on the cross to say He had finished, He was in quite an exceptional degree a sufferer; yet on the cross He was able to say that His suffering also was finished.

Suffering is the reverse side of work. It is the shadow that accompanies achievement, as his shadow follows a man. It is due to the resistance offered to the worker by the medium in which he toils.

The life of Jesus was one of great suffering because He had to do His work in an extremely resistant medium. His purpose was so beneficient, and His passion for the good of the world so obvious, that it might have been expected that He would meet with nothing but encouragement and furtherance. He was so religious that all the religious forces might have been expected to second His efforts; He was so patriotic that it would have been natural if His native country had welcomed Him with open arms; He was so philanthropic that He ought to have been the idol of the multitude. But at every step He met with opposition. Everything that was influential in His age and country turned against Him. Obstruction became more and more persistent and cruel, till at length on Calvary it reached its climax, when all the powers of earth and hell were combined with the one purpose of crushing Him and thrusting Him out of existence. And they succeeded.

But the mystery of suffering is very insufficiently explained when it is defined as the reaction of the work on the worker. While a man's work is what he does with the force of his will, suffering is what is done to him against his will. It may be done by the will of opponents and enemies. But this is never the whole explanation. Above this will, which may be thoroughly evil, there is a will which is good, and means us good by our suffering.

Suffering is the will of God. It is His chief instrument for fashioning His creatures according to His own plan. While by our work we ought to be seeking to make a bit of the world such as He would have it to be, by our suffering He is seeking to make us such as He would have us to be. He blocks up our pathway by it on this side and on that, in order that we may be kept in the path which He has appointed. He prunes our desires and ambitions; He humbles us and makes us meek and acquiescent. By our work we help to make a well-ordered world, but by our suffering He makes a sanctified man; and in His eyes this is by far the greater triumph.

Perhaps this is the most difficult half of life to manage. While it is by no means easy to accomplish the work of life, it is harder still to bear suffering and to benefit by it. Have you ever seen a man to whom nature has given great talents and grace great virtues, so that the possibilities of his life seemed unbounded while he had imagination enough to expatiate over them: a man who might have been a missionary, opening up dark countries to civilization and the Gospel; or a statesman, swaying a parliament with his eloquence and shaping the destinies of millions by his wisdom; or a thinker, wrestling with the problems of his age, sowing the seeds of light, and raising for himself an imperishable monument: but who was laid hold of by some remorseless disease or suddenly crushed by some accident, so that all at once his schemes were upset and his life narrowed to petty anxieties about his health and shifts to avoid the evil day, which could not, however, be long postponed? And did it not seem to you, as you watched him, to be far harder for him to accept this destiny with a good grace and with cheerful submission than it would have been to accomplish the career of enterprise and achievement which once seemed to lie before him? To do nothing is often more difficult than to do the greatest things, and to submit requires more faith than to achieve.

The life of Christ was hemmed and crushed in on every hand. Evil men were the proximate cause of this; but He acknowledged behind them the will of God. He had to accept a career of shame instead of glory, of brief and limited activity instead of far-travelling beneficence, of premature and violent death instead of world-wide and everlasting empire. But He never murmured; however bitter any sacrifice might be on other grounds, He made it sweet to Himself by reflecting that it was the will of His Father. When the worst came to the worst, and He was forced to cry, 'If it be possible, let this cup pass from me', He was swift to add, 'Nevertheless not my will, but thine, be done.' And thus on step after step of the ladder His thoughts were brought into perfect accord with His Father's, and His will was His Father's will.

At last on the cross the cup out of which He had drunk so often was put into His hands for the last time. The draught was large, black and bitter as never before. But He did not flinch. He drank it up. As He did so the last segment of the circle of His own perfection completed itself; and, while flinging the cup away after having exhausted the last drop, He cried, 'It is finished', the echo came back from heaven from those who saw with wonder and adoration the perfect round of His completed character: 'It is finished.'

Though these two sides of the life of Christ are separable in thought, it is evident that they constitute together but one life. (Sometimes they are expressed by saying that life is both a mission and a discipline.) The work He did involved the suffering which He bore, and lent to it meaning and dignity. On the other hand, the suffering perfected the Worker, and thus conferred greatness on His work. In His crowning task of atoning for the sin of the world it was as a sufferer that He accomplished the will of God. And now both are finished; and henceforward the world has a new possession; it has had other perfect things, but never before and never since has it had a perfect life.

SAMUEL CHADWICK (1860-1932)

When only eight years old, Samuel Chadwick started work at the local mill in Burnley, Lancashire, in 1868. He was converted two years later, and became a local preacher in his teens. Discouraged from entering the Methodist ministry, on account of his limited schooling, he became lay pastor of a church at Stacksteads, and when a work of revival began there in 1883 he was accepted as a candidate for the ministry, at Didsbury College, Manchester. He served churches in Edinburgh, Leeds and London before being recalled to Leeds in 1894, as pastor of the huge Oxford Place chapel, where again revival was experienced. He was keenly interested in the Joyful News Training Home, begun by Thomas Champness at Rochdale; and on its transfer in 1903 to Calver, near Sheffield, under the new name of Cliff College, Chadwick became a visiting lecturer; and in 1907 he left Leeds to become resident tutor. In 1912 he was appointed Principal of the College, and Editor of its monthly magazine, *Joyful News*, which was then widely read and esteemed for its teaching on the Spirit-filled life. Some of his articles were collected into books, which became best-sellers. From the most popular of these, *The Way to Pentecost*, chapter five has been selected, 'The Gift of the Holy Ghost', as characteristic of his ministry and writings.

THE GIFT OF THE HOLY GHOST

Pentecost is the crowning miracle and the abiding mystery of grace. It marks the beginning of the Christian dispensation. The tongues of fire sat upon each one of them. The word 'sat' in Scripture marks an end and a beginning. The process of preparation is ended, and the established order has begun. It marks the end of creation, and the beginning of normal forces. 'In six days the Lord made heaven and earth, the sea, and all that in them is, and rested the seventh day.' There is no weariness in God. He did not rest from fatigue. What it means is that all creative work was accomplished. The same figure of speech is used of the Redeemer. Of Him it is said, 'When He had made purification of sins, (He) sat down on the right hand of the Majesty on high.' No other priest had sat down. The priests of the Temple ministered standing, because their ministry was provisional and preparatory, a parable and a prophecy. Christ's own ministry was part of the preparation for the coming of the Spirit. Until He 'sat down' in glory, there could be no dispensation of the Spirit. John says of our Lord's promise in the Temple, 'This spake He of the Spirit, which they that believed on Him were to receive: for the Spirit was not yet given; because Jesus was not yet glorified.' The descent of the One awaited the ascent of the Other. When the work of redemption was complete, the Spirit was given; and when He came He 'sat'. He reigns in the church, as Christ reigns in the heavens. This is the dispensation of the Spirit.

The Holy Ghost is God's gift to the church of His Son. For the work of redemption the Son of God emptied Himself of the prerogatives of His divine status, but for His ministry the Father gave Him the Spirit, and at its close 'He made Him to sit at His right hand in the heavenly sphere, far above all rule, and authority, and power, and dominion, and every name that is named, not only in this world, but also in that which is to come: and He put all things in subjection under His feet, and gave Him to be head over all things to the church which is His body, the fullness of Him that filleth all in all'. Pentecost is the sequel of the Son's investiture. 'Being therefore by the right hand of God exalted, and having received of the Father the promise of the Holy Ghost, He hath poured forth this, which ye see and hear.'

The Spirit in the Church

The sphere of the Spirit is in the living temple of sanctified humanity. He dwells not in temples made with hands. The Temple at Jerusalem was a permitted mistake, as surely as the kingship of Israel. In the New Jerusalem there is no temple. The Tabernacle was a type of heavenly realities. The Temple sought to give solidity, permanence, and magnificence, to that which God meant to be provisional and typical. God cares nothing for costly buildings, and everything for loving hearts. He seeks men. He wants men. He needs men. He dwells in men. Immanuel is the first word and the last of the Gospel of grace. In a powerful plea for the life of prayer, E. M. Bounds says, 'God's plan is to make much of the man, far more of him than of anything else. Men are God's method. The church is looking for better methods; God is looking for better men.' He has staked His kingdom on men. He has trusted His Gospel to men. He has given His Spirit to men. The church is on the stretch for new methods, new plans, new buildings, new organizations, but 'the eyes of the Lord run to and fro throughout the earth, to show Himself strong in the behalf of them whose heart is perfect towards Him'. The Holy Ghost does not come upon methods, but upon men. He does not work through organizations, but through men. He does not dwell in buildings, but in men. He indwells the body of Christ, directs its activities, distributes its forces, empowers its members.

Those gathered in that Upper Room 'when the day of Pentecost was fully come' had been prepared for His coming. They were disciples who acknowledged the Lordship of Jesus. They had realized His saving power, and surrendered all to His sovereign will. For ten days they had been in prayer, and for the greater part of three years they sat at the feet of Jesus. When they realized His Sonship He blessed them, and now the promise of the fiery baptism is fulfilled. The Spirit 'sat upon each one of them; and they were all filled with the Holy Ghost'. He had come to reign over each and all. Jesus Christ had defined His mission, and outlined His programme. He was to unify them into one body, guide them into all truth, and strengthen them for all service. In the church He is the supreme executive, but He has His seat in the soul. He directs all things from the spiritual centre of the inner life. The body prepared for the eternal Son was born of a virgin; the body prepared for the indwelling Spirit is begotten of faith in Jesus Christ, the Son of the living God. The church is the sphere of His ministry, the agent of His purpose, the place of His presence.

The Spirit in the Believer

'The Spirit sat upon each one of them. And they were all filled.'
The whole is for each, and each is for all. The story of Pentecost
reveals what the gift did for individual men, as well as for the whole
company. Peter moves in the blaze of the sun. Throughout the
Gospel narrative he is a man of generous impulses, with many
failings. He utters his resolves with the emphasis of the irresolute,
and often fails in the hour of testing. Pentecost reveals him transformed. He has the certainty of revealed truth in his speech, and the
confidence of invincible power in his bearing. The man who cringed
and sulked a few days ago stands upon both feet, utterly destitute of
fear. Temperament and natural aptitude are unchanged, but the
man is radiant with a new energy, transfigured with a new Spirit,
effective with a new power. The Spirit of Christ has clothed Himself
with Peter. He speaks with the same Galilean accent; but the utterance is of the Holy Ghost. St Paul put the same truth another way
when he said, 'I have been crucified with Christ; yet I live; and yet no
longer I, but Christ liveth in me.' The indwelling Presence is clothed
with sanctified manhood, and becomes the very life of life, and the
very soul of the soul. 'I live; yet no longer I.'

The apostle attributes all spiritual effectiveness to the indwelling
power. 'Our sufficiency', he says, 'is of God, who also hath made us
able ministers of the new testament: not of the letter, but of the
spirit; for the letter killeth, but the spirit giveth life.' There are other
kinds of ability than that which comes of God through the Spirit, but
they are death-dealing and never life-giving. It is the Spirit that
quickens. Everything else fails. The letter may be faultlessly orthodox, the method may be marvellously ingenious, the man may be
tremendously earnest, but only the God-made, God-inspired, God-
enabled avails. Carnalities kill. The power that quickens, transforms, perfects, is of God the Spirit. There never was so much
human perfection in the church, but the New Jerusalem is not built
up by the power of Babylon; it comes down out of heaven from God.
Believers without the Holy Ghost cannot do the work of the Spirit.

The Spirit in the World

It is this mystery that has filled the history of the church with
anomalies. Inadequate men are always doing impossible things, and
ordinary men achieve extraordinary results. God's biggest things
seem to be done by the most unlikely people. Unknown Davids kill
terrifying Goliaths. The weak confound the mighty, and things hid
from the learned and wise are made known to unlearned and

ignorant men. The All-wise seems to delight in nothing so much as turning the wisdom of the vain to folly, and the strength of the proud to shame. He has declared the insufficiency of all but Himself, but man struts and sets himself to demonstrate his own sufficiency. Pride of logic, pride of skill, pride of personality, pride of power, perpetuate the spirit of Babel in the church of God, with the same inevitable result. It ends in defeat, disaster, and dishonour. There is no conquest of the world for God but by the Holy Ghost. He alone can convict the world 'in respect of sin, and of righteousness, and of judgment'. There is no other power that can do that, and without conviction there can be neither the salvation of the soul nor the coming of the Kingdom. Our one lack is the power that comes of the Spirit. For holiness and for service, for prosperity and for victory, He is our one need. The Spirit is God's gift. The power cannot be bought either with money or merit. A gift can only be received or rejected. The gift is for all who believe and crown Jesus Christ in their hearts.

SAMUEL LOGAN BRENGLE (1860-1936)

The Salvation Army's foremost exponent of its teaching on holiness and the 'clean heart'—the expulsion of all sinful propensities and desires, through the power of the indwelling Holy Spirit—Commissioner Samuel Logan Brengle, DD, OF, was an American. Born into a godly family in Indiana, he trained for the Methodist ministry and was a student-pastor when, in 1885, he heard William Booth preach, and determined to join the Salvation Army. He married one of its officers, and journeyed to England for training as an officer. His speaking and writing on holiness attracted attention, and led to his appointment in 1897 as 'spiritual special' officer. He travelled widely to conduct holiness meetings. His best-known book, *The Way of Holiness*, was written at the behest of General Bramwell Booth, William Booth's son and successor, in 1902. The following first two chapters are typical examples of his writings.

WHAT IS HOLINESS?

A number of years ago a girl asked me, 'What is this sanctification, or holiness, that people are talking so much about?' She had heard the experience testified to and preached about for nearly a year, until I thought that, of course, she understood it. Her question surprised and almost discouraged me, but I rallied and asked, 'Have you a bad temper?'

'Oh, yes,' she said, 'I have a temper like a volcano.'

'Sanctification,' I replied, 'is to have that bad temper taken out.' That definition set her thinking and did her good; but it was hardly accurate. If I had said, 'Sanctification is to have our sinful tempers cleansed, and the heart filled with love to God and man', that would have done, for that is sanctification, that is holiness. It is, in our measure, to be made like God. It is to be made 'partakers of the divine nature' (2 Pet. 1.4).

A spark from the fire is like the fire. The tiniest twig on the giant oak, or the smallest branch of the vine, has the nature of the oak or the vine, and is in that respect like the oak or the vine. A drop of water on the end of your finger from the ocean is like the ocean: not in its size, of course, for the big ships cannot float upon it nor the big fishes swim in it; but it is like the ocean in its essence, in its character, in its nature. Just so, a holy person is like God. Not that he is infinite as God is; he does not know everything; he has not all power and wisdom as God has; but he is like God in his nature. He is good and pure and loving and just, in the same way that God is.

Holiness, then, is conformity to the nature of God. It is likeness to God as He is revealed in Jesus.

But some one will cry out, 'Impossible! We are poor sinful creatures. We cannot be like Jesus. He was divine. Show me 'a man like Jesus Christ.'

Well, now, let us go to the Bible and see what that says about the matter before we further define holiness. What did Jesus Himself say?

1. In speaking of the separation of His disciples from the world, Jesus says, 'They are not of the world, even as I am not of the world.' And again, 'As Thou hast sent me into the world, even so have I also sent them into the world' (John 17. 16, 18). We are, then, to be like Jesus in separation from the world. Jesus was in the world but He was

not of the world. He took no pleasure in its wicked ways. He was not spoiled at all by its proud, sinful, selfish spirit. While He worked and associated with bad people to do them good, yet He was always separate from them in spirit.

One of our dear, good rescue officers went to a brothel to see a sick girl. While she was there the health authorities declared the girl's sickness to be smallpox, and sealed up the place. The officer was shut in for weeks among those poor lost women. She was in an evil place but she was not of it. Her pure spirit was utterly opposed to the spirit of sin that ruled there. So Jesus was in the world but not of it; and in the same way, holy people are so changed that while they are in the world they are not of it. They belong to heaven and are but strangers and pilgrims, doing all the good they can while passing through this world to their Father's house, their heavenly home. They are separate from the world.

2. The Apostle John, in speaking of those who expect to see Jesus and to be like Him in heaven says, 'And every man that hath this hope in Him purifieth himself, even as He is pure' (1 John 3.3). That is a lofty standard of purity, for there was no impurity in Jesus. He allowed no unclean habits. He indulged in no impure thoughts or desires. He used no unkind words. He kept Himself pure in all things. So we are to be pure in heart and in life as He was.

3. Again, Jesus said, in speaking of God's kindness and love for unjust and evil people, 'Be ye therefore perfect, even as your Father which is in heaven is perfect' (Matt. 5.48).

Again, He says, 'A new commandment I give unto you, that ye love one another.' How? According to what standard? 'As I have loved you, that ye also love one another' (John 13.34). We are, then, to be like Jesus in love to God and to all men, even to our enemies, but especially to our brothers and sisters in the Lord.

4. In speaking of Himself, Jesus says, 'Believe me that I am in the Father, and the Father in me' (John 14.11). And then He says of His disciples, 'At that day' (the day of Pentecost when the Comforter comes) 'ye shall know that I am in my Father, and ye in me, and I in you' (John 14.20). We are, then, to be like Jesus by having God dwelling in us.

So we see that the Bible teaches that we can be like Jesus. We are to be like Him in our separation from the world, in purity, in love, and in the fullness of the Spirit. This is holiness.

The work was begun in you when you were converted. You gave up your sins. You were in some measure separated from the world, the love of God was in some degree shed abroad in your heart, and you felt that God was with you. But unless you have been sanctified wholly, you also feel that there are yet roots of bitterness within: quickness of temper, stirrings of pride, too great a sensitiveness to praise or blame, shame of the cross, love of ease, worldly-mindedness, and the like. These must be taken away before your heart can be made clean, love to God and man made perfect, and the Holy Spirit have all His way in you. When this is done, you will have the experience which the Bible calls holiness, and which the Salvation Army rightly teaches is the birthright of all God's dear children.

Holiness, then, for you and for me, is not maturity, but purity; a clean heart in which the Holy Spirit dwells, filling it with pure, tender, and constant love to God and man.

There is a plant in South America called the 'pitcher plant', on the stalk of which, below each leaf, is a little cup-like formation which is always full of water. When it is very small it is full; as it grows larger it is still full; and when it reaches maturity it is full. That illustrates holiness. All that God asks is that the heart should be cleansed from sin and full of love, whether it be the tender heart of the little child with feeble powers of loving, or the full-grown man, or the flaming archangel before the throne. This is holiness, and this only. It is nothing less than this, and it can be nothing more.

> Jesus, Thine all-victorious love
>   Shed in my heart abroad;
> Then shall my feet no longer rove,
>   Rooted and fixed in God.

*　　*　　*

WHY SHOULD WE BE HOLY?

We should be holy because God wants us to be holy. He commands it. He says, 'As He which hath called you is holy, so be ye holy in all manner of conversation; because it is written, Be ye holy; for I am holy' (1 Pet. 1. 15–16). God is in earnest about this. It is God's will and it cannot be evaded. Just as a man wants his watch to keep perfect time, his work to be accurate, wants his friends to be steadfast, his children to be obedient, his wife to be faithful, so God wants us to be holy.

To many, however, the command seems harsh. They have been accustomed to commands accompanied by curses or kicks or blows. But we must not forget that 'God is love', and His commands are not harsh but kind. They come from the fullness of an infinitely loving and all-wise heart. They are meant for our good. If a railway train could think or talk, it might argue that running on two rails over the same road year after year was very common-place. But if it insisted on larger liberty and jumped the track, it would certainly ruin itself. So the man who wants freedom, and refuses to obey God's commands to be holy, destroys himself. The train was made to run on the track, and we were made to live according to God's commandment to be holy. Only in that way can we gain everlasting good.

Oh, how tender are His words! 'And now . . . what doth the Lord thy God require of thee, but to fear the Lord thy God, to walk in all His ways, and to love Him, and to serve the Lord thy God with all thy heart and with all thy soul, to keep the commandments of the Lord, and His statutes . . . for thy good?' (Deut. 10. 12–13).

For thy good! Do you not see it, my brother, my sister? It is 'for thy good'. There is nothing harsh, nothing selfish in our dear Lord's command. It is 'thy good' He is seeking. Bless His name! 'God is love.'

We should be holy because Jesus died to make us holy. He gave Himself to stripes and spitting and cruel mockings, the crown of thorns and death on the cross for this purpose. He wants a holy people. For this He prayed. 'Sanctify them through Thy truth: Thy word is truth' (John 17.17). For this He died. 'Who gave Himself for us, that He might redeem us from all iniquity, and purify unto Himself a peculiar people, zealous of good works' (Titus 2.14). He 'loved the church, and gave Himself for it; that He might sanctify and cleanse it . . . that He might present it to Himself a glorious church, not having spot, or wrinkle, or any such thing; but that it should be holy and without blemish' (Eph. 5.25–27). Let us not disappoint Him. Let not His precious blood be spent in vain.

We should be holy in order that we may be made useful. Who have been the mightiest men of God in all the ages? They have been holy men; men with clean hearts on fire with love to God and man; unselfish men; humble men who forgot themselves in their love and toil for others; faithful men whose lives were 'hid with Christ in God'. Moses, the meekest of men; Paul, who would gladly pour out his life a sacrifice for the people; Luther, Fox, St Francis, Wesley, General and Mrs Booth, and ten thousand times ten thousand other men and women who were 'great in the sight of the Lord'. These are the ones whom God has used.

So long as there are any roots of sin in the heart the Holy Spirit cannot have all His way in us, and our usefulness is hindered. But when our hearts are clean the Holy Spirit dwells within, and then we have power for service. Then we can work for God, and do good in spite of all our ignorance and weakness. Hallelujah!

A plain, humble young Irishman heard about the blessing of a clean heart, and went alone and fell on his knees before the Lord, crying to Him for it. A man happened to overhear him and wrote about it, saying, 'I shall never forget his petition. "O God, I plead with Thee for this blessing." Then, as if God was showing him what was in the way, he said, "My Father, I will give up every known sin, only I plead with Thee for power." And then, as if his individual sins were passing before him, he said again and again, "I will give them up; I will give them up." Then without any emotion he rose from his knees, turned his face heavenward, and simply said, "And now I claim the blessing." For the first time he now became aware of my presence and, with a shining face, reached out his hand to clasp mine. You could feel the presence of the Spirit as he said, "I have received Him; I have received Him!" And I believe he had, for in the next few months he led more than sixty men into the Kingdom of God. His whole life was transformed.'

To be holy and useful is possible for each one of us, and is far better than to be great and famous. To save a soul is better than to command an army, to win a battle, to rule an empire or to sit upon a throne.

Again, we should be holy that we may be safe. Sin in the heart is more dangerous than gunpowder in the cellar. Before the disciples got the blessing of a clean heart and the baptism of the Holy Spirit they forsook their Master and fled.

Remember that holiness is nothing more nor less than perfect love for God and man in a clean heart. If we love God with all our heart we will gladly keep all His commandments and do all His will as He makes it known to us. And if we love our fellow-men as we love ourselves, we will not do, knowingly, any wrong to them. So we see that this holy love is the surest possible safeguard against all kinds of sin either against God or man, and we cannot count ourselves safe unless we have it. Without it, Peter and David fell; but with it, Joseph and Daniel resisted the temptations of kings' courts, and the three Hebrew children and the fire-baptized Stephen and Paul gladly faced death rather than deny their Lord.

Finally, we should be holy because we are most solemnly assured that without holiness 'no man shall see the Lord' (Heb. 12.14). God has made all things ready so that we may have the blessing if we will, thus leaving those who refuse or trifle and fail without excuse.

I bless Him that years ago He awakened me to the infinite

importance of this matter, sent holy people to testify to and explain the experience, enabled me to consecrate my whole being to Him and seek Him with all my heart, and gave me the blessing.

Will you have it, my comrade? If so, receive Jesus as your Sanctifier just now.

> My idols I cast at Thy feet,
>   My all I return Thee, who gave!
> This moment the work is complete,
>   For thou art almighty to save!
>
> O Saviour, I dare to believe,
>   Thy blood for my cleansing I see;
> And, asking in faith, I receive
>   Salvation, full, present, and free.

G. CAMPBELL MORGAN (1863-1945)

One of the outstanding expository preachers of the twentieth century, George Campbell Morgan was the son of a Baptist minister, and began preaching at the age of 13. While still at school, and then as a teacher — first in a Wesleyan Methodist school, and afterwards at a Jewish school, where he learned much from its rabbi headmaster — he participated enthusiastically in tent and other evangelistic missions. Nevertheless he was rejected as a candidate for the Wesleyan Methodist ministry. His powers as a preacher, however, in 1883 attracted the attention of D. L. Moody, with whom he established a close and lasting friendship. In 1889 he was ordained to the ministry of the Congregational church, and held three brief pastorates before his memorable ministry at Westminster Chapel, London, 1904–17, during which he was also President of Cheshunt College, Cambridge, 1911–14. He travelled extensively, in an itinerant ministry, on both sides of the Atlantic, 1919–32, and in 1933 returned to Westminster Chapel for a further notable period, until his death. His extensive literary output was based mainly upon reported sermons. This superb chapter on the Incarnation is from *Crises of the Christ* (published by Pickering and Inglis).

THE GREAT MYSTERY — THE GOD-MAN

The subject of the Incarnation is at once initial and fundamental. The Lord Jesus Christ is a Person infinitely transcending the possibility of perfect human comprehension. Nevertheless the Scripture declares certain facts concerning Him, which account for His glory and His grace, and without which He remains an unsolved problem, defying every successive age in its attempts to account for Him. It should at once be admitted that no final words of explanation can be written concerning Him. And yet it is of the utmost importance that so much as has been revealed should be recognized, in order to have a comprehension of the true meaning of His mission.

In the later letters of the Apostle Paul, notably that to the Colossians, it is evident that he is supremely anxious that Christian people should know Christ. In declaring this he expresses the thought in the words, 'That they may know the mystery of God, even Christ' (Col. 2.2). He speaks of Christ as 'the mystery of God'. It will be of value to understand the New Testament use and meaning of the word 'mystery'. That has been most lucidly stated to be 'a truth undiscoverable except by revelation: never necessarily (as our popular use of the word may suggest) a thing unintelligible or perplexing in itself. In Scripture a mystery may be a fact which, when revealed, we cannot understand in detail, though we can know it and act upon it. . . . It is a thing only to be known when revealed' (Bishop Handley Moule).

In this sense Christ is the mystery of God. Perfect analysis and explanation of His Person is impossible. The fact thereof is declared as to the origin and essential characteristics. These must be recognized, in order to a right understanding of the great subject of human redemption.

Having seen that reconstruction in the region of destruction was utterly impossible, that there is no way, in the wisdom or power of man, for the encompassing of his own restoration, it was to be expected that the divine method of redemption would be beyond perfect explanation to the sons of men. That which human wisdom cannot plan must necessarily be beyond its power perfectly to understand. Human intelligence is capable of appreciating anything that lies within the range of the working of human wisdom. The intelligence of one man may not be equal to the discovery of the method of transmitting words by electricity without use of wires. When, however, another human intelligence has thought the matter out, this man is able to comprehend the explanation given. It may therefore be argued that while man was not equal in his own wisdom to devising a plan of redemption, he ought to be able perfectly to comprehend the plan of God. Yet this does not follow. In the first case the whole movement is within the compass of human intelligence. In the second, all human wisdom has been utterly exhausted in its attempt to think of, or to discover a method of salvation, and has failed. The failure, moreover, must have continued through all the ages, for the Person of Christ, and the whole scheme of human redemption, are so transcendently marvellous as to demand for their explanation the recognition of their divine origin. All this is to emphasize a fact that must not be lost sight of in approaching the contemplation of this initial movement of God towards man, that while the great facts are declared, they cannot be perfectly comprehended by human reason; and it is necessary therefore to approach them in the attitude of faith.

These statements apply with equal force to the whole mystery of the life, and death, and resurrection of Jesus. The subject is therefore to be approached with holy and submissive reverence. The attitude of the mind in its approach is defined in words spoken long centuries ago for the children of Israel, by Moses the servant of God: 'The secret things belong unto Jehovah our God; but the things that are revealed belong to us and to our children for ever, that we may do all the words of this law' (Deut. 29.29). There are secret things which belong unto the Lord. There are revealed things which God has made so plain that they may be comprehended: these 'belong unto us and to our children'. It is the solemn duty of all who desire to know the Christ, that they should diligently study the things revealed, and reverently rest with regard to the secret things.

The present study is devoted chiefly to the birth of Christ, as the crisis of Incarnation. There is always the danger of dwelling more upon the birth of the human, than of contemplating that birth as the crisis through which God became incarnate. It is in the latter way, however, that the subject is now to be approached, and in the following order. First, *the testimony of Scripture*; second, *the mystery as to the secret things*; third, *the mystery revealed*.

I. From the great mass of declaration in the New Testament concerning this subject, it will be sufficient to take four principal passages. These will again be divided into, first, annunciations to be reverently read, and received without attempted explanation; and secondly, doctrinal declarations to be reverently considered.

The annunciations are those of the angel to Joseph and to Mary. In connection with the latter it will be necessary also to read the brief historic statement concerning the fulfilment of the angelic message.

The annunciation to Joseph was uttered in these words, 'Joseph, thou son of David, fear not to take unto thee Mary thy wife; for that which is conceived in her is of the Holy Spirit. And she shall bring forth a son; and thou shalt call His name JESUS; for it is He that shall save His people from their sins. Now all this is come to pass that it might be fulfilled which was spoken by the Lord through the prophet, saying:

> Behold, the virgin shall be with child, and
>   shall bring forth a son,
> And they shall call His name Immanuel;

which is, being interpreted, God with us' (Matt. 1.20–23, RV).

In the presence of this mysterious announcement there can be no fitting attitude of the human intellect save that of acceptance of the truth, without any attempt to explain the absolute mystery. The annunciation reveals the fact that in the origin of the Person of Jesus there was the co-operation of deity and humanity, each making its own contribution.

The annunication to Mary should be read in close connection with the statement of its fulfilment in history. 'And the angel answered and said unto her, The Holy Spirit shall come upon thee, and the power of the Most High shall overshadow thee, wherefore also the holy thing which is born of thee shall be called the Son of God. . . . And she brought forth her first-born son; and she wrapped Him in swaddling clothes, and laid Him in a manger, because there was no room for them in the inn' (Luke 1.35; 2.7). This annunciation and declaration concerned one Person, spoken of in the former as the Son of God, in the latter as 'her son'. Here are not two persons, but one.

These annunciations are to be read and received without any attempt to explain the central mystery contained within them, which absolutely transcends all human understanding. They must be received, or else the whole superstructure of Christianity totters and falls. It is only by the way of the fact here declared, that it is at all possible to comprehend the great facts which are evident in the whole subsequent work of this Person. To deny the truth of this account of the initial crisis, is to be left to the contemplation of effects for which no sufficient cause can be found. The stupendous and ever manifest combination in the Personality of Jesus of essential deity, and proper humanity, is totally without sufficient cause the moment men have ceased to have faith in the Scripture account of the miraculous conception. The initial miracle cannot be finally explained, but neither can the origin of any form of life be finally explained in the last analysis.

The doctrinal declarations to be considered are those of John and of Paul. That of John is in the introduction to his Gospel: 'And the Word became flesh, and dwelt among us . . . full of grace and truth' (John 1.14). For the sake of the present consideration, the parenthetical declaration, 'and we beheld His glory, glory as of the only begotten from the Father', is omitted. To rightly appreciate the meaning of this statement it is necessary to connect it with the opening words of the Gospel: 'In the beginning was the Word, and the Word was with God, and the Word was God' (John 1.1). The passage from the second to the thirteenth verse inclusive, is a statement giving parenthetically the history of the Word from the beginning of the first creation, to the beginning of the second.

Omitting this passage, verses 1 and 14, read in immediate connection, contain a declaration of the sublimest facts concerning the Person of Christ, and a statement of His coming into relation with the human race in the mystery of Incarnation. In each of these passages there is a threefold statement, and they answer to each other.

'In the beginning was the Word.'	'And the Word became flesh.'
'And the Word was with God.'	'And tabernacled among us.'
'And the Word was God.'	'Full of grace and truth.'

This is a statement of the mystery of the Incarnation, a setting in doctrinal form of that fact, announced by heavenly messengers to Joseph and to Mary.

The first statement is full of a majesty and sublimity which flings its light about the pathway, but which cannot be penetrated or perfectly comprehended. 'In the beginning was the Word.' The phrase 'in the beginning' in this connection antedates any other reference to the ages to be found in the sacred volume. By it man is borne back into the infinite and unfathomable reaches of the unmeasurable. The phrase with which the book of Genesis opens takes man to the beginning of the history of the present order, to those original movements of the divine mind and power by which material things originated. The phrase as John uses it, in these opening words, carries the mind yet again beyond those original movements of creation. By its aid the mind of man is introduced to the presence of the Self-existent God. Contemplating the unutterable splendour, whose very light darkens the understanding of the finite mind, the Word is found existing. A word is a means of expression. The word of man is man's method of self-expression. The Word of God is the name here used for that Person in the Trinity who is the divine method of self-expression.

'The Word became flesh.' The statement is appalling, overwhelming. Out of the infinite distances, into the finite nearness; from the unknowable to the knowable; from the method of self-expression appreciable by deity alone, to a method of self-expression understandable of the human.

In the inscrutable mystery of the Trinity the Son is ever the medium of self-expression. By this awe-inspiring fact of Incarnation, the office of the Son is not changed. Its method is changed for the sake of man. The movement of the change no human intelligence can follow. It is darkly mysterious with the darkness of a blinding splendour. The conception is too mighty ever to have been born in the intelligence of man. 'The Word which was in the beginning . . . became flesh.'

'The Word was with God.' The natural home of the eternal Son, who was the medium of self-revelation of deity, was in close fellowship with the eternal Father. 'The Word tabernacled among us', that is, took up His manifest dwelling-place in proximity to the human race, as close as that which characterized His relation to the eternal Father. He stooped into an actual identification with human nature, and by that stoop lifted human nature into the spaciousness of fellowship with God.

This, however, let it be stated in advance, is not the doctrine of Atonement. In the Person of Jesus, God has come into new and mystic relationship with unfallen humanity; and in the life of Jesus, God in relation with unfallen humanity, tabernacles among fallen men. Something more will be necessary to make possible union between the members of a fallen race, and this new Head of an unfallen race. That something more will be accomplished by the way of the cross.

'And the Word was God.' The final declaration is that of the supreme deity of the Word, and thus the Person of Christ is safeguarded from any interpretation which would place Him in infinite superiority to the human race, and yet in inferiority to essential deity. He was God, and yet in His Person there was not all the truth concerning God, for He was with God. He was with God, and yet by no means inferior to the eternal Father, for He was God. The unity of deity is marked by the word 'God'. The diversity is marked by 'the Word'. The God who created, the Word was with. In the revelation of Incarnation, the phrase answering this final sentence is 'full of grace and truth'. This teaches that in the grace or loveliness, and truth or righteousness of the Man seen of John and the rest, there was an outshining of the essential facts of the love and the light of deity.

In the statement of Paul the same great truths are affirmed in other language. From the passage in Philippians in which the humiliation and exaltation of Christ are so splendidly set forth, let the words be taken which deal immediately with this fact. 'Who, existing in the form of God, counted not the being on an equality with God a thing to be grasped, but emptied Himself, taking the form of a servant, being made in the likeness of men' (Phil. 2.6-7). In this passage there is first stated the eternal fact concerning Christ 'existing in the form of God'. Then follows the attitude of the mind of the eternal Word, in the presence of the call for redemption. He 'counted not the being on an equality with God a thing to be grasped'. Then follows the sublime act through which He came to the level of those needing succour. He 'emptied Himself, taking the form of a servant, being made in the likeness of men'. Carefully note three facts in the compass of this brief passage. First, it declares the eternal verity concerning Christ. He existed in the form of God, on an equality with God. Second, it reveals the position He took, when He came for the redemption of man. He took the form of a servant in the likeness of men. In these two there is a contrast. Take the extreme statements, and He is seen as passing from the form of God to the likeness of men; and taking the nearer contrast, He is seen as passing from the sovereignty of equality to the submission of subservience.

The third fact is the revelation of the attitude of mind, and the act of will, by which this change was wrought. In the presence of a great need He did not hold to, or grasp His right of equality, but for the accomplishment of an infinite purpose, abandoned this. The action of the will is declared in the sublime and all-inclusive declaration that 'He emptied Himself'. The eternal Word stooped from the position of an infinite expression to the limitations of human life.

It is now of the utmost importance to understand what is involved in the declaration that He emptied Himself. There is no warrant for imagining that He emptied Himself of His essential deity. The emptying indicates the setting aside of one form of manifestation, in which all the facts of equality with God were evidently revealed, for another form of manifestation, in which the fact of equality with

God must for a time be hidden by the necessary submissiveness of the human to the divine. That which the eternal Word set aside was a form, and this in order that another form might be taken. It is evident, therefore, that a very great deal depends upon the meaning of the word 'form'.

The Greek word, *morphe*, occurs only in one other place in the whole of the New Testament. In speaking of an appearance of Christ after resurrection, Mark says, 'After these things He was manifested in another form unto two of them, as they walked, on their way into the country' (Mark 16.12). Taking this use of the word for the sake of illustration, it is evident that the change was not in the essential nature or personality, but in the method of manifestation. To the men who walked to Emmaus the same One came, but in a changed form, so that they did not recognize Him until He willed to reveal His identity. This of course by comparison with the subject now under consideration was but a small change, and yet it serves to illustrate the larger fact.

In the coming of the eternal Word to the earth for the purposes of redemption, He did not lay aside the essential fact of His deity; He simply changed the form of manifestation. It would seem clearly evident that the Son of God had for ever been the One in whom God took form, and therefore the One through whom God was revealed. The Son is always the manifestation of the Father. What the form, what the manifestation was in the past, it is impossible to declare, for it is beyond the comprehension of the finite and the limited. This alone is certain: that He was the Word, the Speech, the Method of communication of the eternal God. For the redemption of man He laid aside that form, whatever it may have been, and took a new form for manifesting the same God, a form upon which men might look, and through which, in the process of time, they might come to know the eternal God. If it were possible for a moment to penetrate the mysteries of the past, the Son would be seen within the mystery of the Trinity as the perpetual medium of divine expression, just as the Spirit is the perpetual medium of divine consciousness. In the coming to the level of man, and in the taking of a form possible of comprehension by man, it was necessary to bring the illimitable range into the range of the limited. He passed from the heavenly to the earthly, from the infinite to the finite, that is, as to form of expression. This is impossible of final explanation. It is however a mystery revealed, upon which the whole superstructure of Christianity depends. It would seem as though the eternal heavens were for a period emptied of the manifestation of God, though never of His presence, while for the work of redemption God was manifest in the flesh.

The Word passed from government to obedience; from independent co-operation in the equality of deity, to dependent submission to the will of God. By the way of the Incarnation there came into existence a Person in all points human, in all essentials divine. In all points human, that is to say, fulfilling the divine ideal of human nature, not descending to the level of the degradation of humanity resulting from sin. The Man of Nazareth was perfect as man. He was, moreover, perfect as God, lacking nothing of the powers of essential deity, save only the heavenly form of manifestation.

II. At this point the temptation is to ask questions. These may be asked, but they cannot be answered. Here is the sphere in which faith becomes operative, for here the mystery is seen as to its secret things which belong to God. How can there be united in one Person, perfect and complete deity, and perfect and complete humanity? It is impossible to reply to the 'how?' Will not these things, however, so contradict each other as to make both impossible? The only answer is that they did not, and that through all the life of Jesus there were constantly manifested the essential and absolute nature of deity, and the undoubted facts of humanity. There are no essentials of human nature that cannot be discovered in the story of this Person. His spiritual nature is evidenced by His unceasing recognition of God. His mental capacity is manifest in the marvellous majesty of His dealing with all problems. His physical life is seen moving along the line of the purely human in its hunger, its weariness, its method of sustenance, and its seasons of rest. The human will is seen, but always choosing, as the principle of activity, the divine will. The emotional nature is manifest in the tears and the tenderness, the rebuke and the anger, gleaming with soft light, flaming as the lightning. The intellectual nature is seen so perfectly balanced, and so wonderfully equipped, that men marvelled at His wisdom, seeing, as they said, that He had never learned.

Yet, moreover, the essentials of deity are seen. Such wisdom, that the ages have failed to understand perfectly the deep meaning of His teaching. Such power, that through weakness He operated towards the accomplishment of works that were only possible to God. Such love, that attempts to describe it but rob it of its fairest glory.

And yet again, in this Person is seen the merging of the divine and the human, until one wonders where is the ending of the one and the beginning of the other. Denouncing and proclaiming doom upon guilty Jerusalem, the voice is yet choked with emotion, and the face is wet with tears. That is surely human. And yet it is essentially divine, for while the expression of the emotion is human as all tears are, the emotion expressed is divine, for none but God can mingle the doom of the guilty with the tears of a great pity.

It would seem as though there were no adequate naming of this Personality, but that created by the combination of the two names in one. He was the God-man. Not God indwelling a man. Of such there have been many. Not a man deified. Of such there have been none save in the myths of pagan systems of thought. But God and man, combining in one Personality the two natures, a perpetual enigma and mystery, baffling the possibility of explanation. It may be asked how, if indeed He were God, He could be tempted in the realm of humanity, as other men are tempted. It may be objected that had He been God, He could not have spoken of the limitation of His own knowledge concerning things to come. When asked to explain these things, the only possible answer is that they do not admit of explanation, but they remain facts, proving His essential humanity; while on the other hand are the incontrovertible proofs of His deity, in the activity of raising the dead, and in the matchless wisdom of His teaching, and supremely in the revelation of God which has taken hold of, and influenced the whole conception of deity during the passing of the centuries since His life upon earth.

This mystery and revelation uniting God and man in a Person is the centre of Christianity, and is without parallel, and without possibility of explanation by analogy.

It has been objected that this is the creation of the imagination of men. This however is to presuppose the possibility of an exercise of the imagination to which it is wholly unequal. Imagination can only rearrange known facts. The poems of the poet may be new, and the picture of the artist also, but in each case upon examination they will be found to be new in their combination and representation of old facts. The union in a Person of God and man was something undreamed of, unknown, until it broke upon the world as a fact in human history.

III. In the Gospels there are three expressions descriptive of Jesus Christ which are suggestive of the double fact in His personality, a contemplation of which will aid in the study of the revealed mystery. The first of them, 'the Son of God', indicates the deity of Jesus, and yet perfectly describes His humanity. The second, 'the Son of man', indicates His relation to the race, and yet ever suggests that separateness from it which was created by the fact of His deity. The third, 'the Son', always suggests the union of these facts in the unity of His Person. An examination of the four Gospels, and a selection from them of the passages in which these titles occur, reveal certain facts of interest concerning them.

Taking them in order, the term, 'the Son of God', occurs in Matthew, nine times; in Mark, four times; in Luke, six times; and in John, eleven times. The title in Matthew is never used by Christ Himself, six times it is the language of men, and three times that of devils. In the Gospel of Mark it is never used by Christ, but by men twice, by devils twice. In the Gospel of Luke it is never used by Christ, but by an angel once, by a man once, and by devils four times. In the Gospel of John the title is on five occasions used by Jesus, and six times by men. It is interesting to note that in the three Gospels dealing principally with the humanity of Jesus, He is never recorded as having spoken of Himself as the Son of God. In the one Gospel of His deity, He is recorded as having used the expression five times. About one of these there is a doubt, for it is not at all certain whether the words, 'He that believeth on Him is not judged; but he that believeth not hath been judged already, because he hath not believed on the name of the only begotten Son of God' (John 3.18), do not form part of John's commentary, rather than of the actual discourse of Jesus. Four times that are certain, indicate a method and a reason. Twice He so described Himself in answering His critics (John 5.25; 10.36), once when He brought comfort and light to an excommunicated man (John 9.35), and once when He would succour two broken-hearted women, whose brother Lazarus He was about to raise from the dead (John 11.4).

The term, 'Son of man', occurs in Matthew thirty-two times, in Mark fifteen times, in Luke twenty-six times, and in John twelve times. In the first three Gospels, the title is always recorded as having been used by Christ of Himself, and never by angel, by man, or by demon. Of the twelve occasions in John, ten are from the lips of Christ, twice only was the expression used by man, and then in the spirit of criticism and unbelief: 'We have heard out of the law that the Christ abideth for ever; and how sayest Thou, the Son of man must be lifted up? Who is this Son of man?' (John 12.34).

The last of these expressions, 'the Son', the greatest of the three, without either qualifying phrase, and therefore suggesting both relationships, occurs in Matthew four times, in Mark once, in Luke three times, and in John fifteen times. Without a single exception the phrase is used by Christ Himself, never by angel, or man, or demon.

This rapid survey shows that Christ's favourite expression for describing Himself is the one which veiled His glory, 'the Son of man'. He most often described Himself in a way in which men never describe Him, save when, repeating His own language, they in doubt ask what He meant. He also used, and He alone, the expression, 'the Son', suggesting in the light of the other two expressions, His relation to the divine, and His relation to the human. The expression which declared His essential glory only passed His lips, in all probability, four times.

The value of this examination of the use of the descriptive phrases may thus be stated. He was the Son of God, but that great fact never passed His lips save when some pressing circumstance made it necessary that for rebuke or comfort He should declare the eternal relationship which He bore to God. The title which He seems to have loved best was that which marked His humanity, and His relationship to the race, 'the Son of man'. Occasionally, and always under circumstances of special need, He spoke of Himself as 'the Son'.

These very titles suggest the essential fact concerning Him. At the birth of Jesus of Nazareth there came into existence one Personality such as, with reference to the duality of His nature, had never had existence before. The Son of God came from the eternities. The Son of man began His being. The Son, combining the two facts in one Personality, commenced that mighty work which He alone could accomplish, bringing to its carrying out all the forces of deity, in union with the capacities of humanity.

W. GRAHAM SCROGGIE (1877-1958)

Although proud of his Scottish ancestry, and cherishing his Scottish accent, William Graham Scroggie was born and educated in England. His father was an evangelist, and Graham grew up among the Brethren. He entered Spurgeon's College at the age of 19, and had a distressing experience at his first two churches, being obliged to leave one because of 'Modernist' influences among the congregation, and the other because of his stand against 'worldliness'. There followed ten fruitful years at Bethesda Chapel, Sunderland, and his most memorable ministry, for 17 years, at Charlotte Chapel, Edinburgh, during which the University of Edinburgh conferred upon him an honorary Doctorate of Divinity. Two years of travelling in Australia and America were followed by seven years at the Metropolitan (Spurgeon's) Tabernacle, London, until his retirement from pastoral responsibility in 1944. Regarded as his generation's foremost Bible teacher on the Keswick Convention platform, he gave series of Bible Readings there twelve times — a record in the Convention's history. He wrote many books, but none exemplifies his expository style better than the Keswick Convention address on 'Purposing and Accomplishing', delivered in 1946.

PURPOSING AND ACCOMPLISHING

They went forth to go into the land of Canaan; and into the land of Canaan they came (Genesis 12.5).

This striking statement of an event which occurred in the Middle East, 3,800 years ago, has an unmistakable significance for us today; so let us examine it. The passage speaks of a divine revelation, a momentous resolution, and a joyful realization.

There is, first, *a divine revelation*. In these few words, 'the land of Canaan' is spoken of twice, and the 'land' is the revelation, both geographically and spiritually. God said to Abram, 'Get thee out of thy country *unto a land that I will show thee*', and its spiritual counterpart is also a subject of revelation.

The whole history of the chosen people has its spiritual application. The people in Egypt tell of men as subjects of Satan's kingdom, oppressed and wretched. The deliverance of the people through the Red Sea tells of that emancipation of men which takes place at the time of their regeneration. The passage through the Jordan tells of the regenerated man's identification with Christ in His death and resurrection. The wilderness wandering tells of the experience of those Christians who get stuck between Calvary and Pentecost. And 'the land of Canaan' tells of that experience of rest and victory which is entered into, here and now, by faith. 'We who have believed *do* enter into *that rest*.'

As Canaan was the sphere of Israel's life, so 'the heavenlies' is the sphere of the believer's life. As Canaan was the place of Israel's conflict, so 'the heavenlies' is the place where the Christian wrestles with wicked spirits. And as Canaan was the land of Israel's wealth, so the believer is 'blessed with every spiritual blessing in the heavenlies in Christ'. It is a mistake to interpret Jordan as the passage of death, and Canaan as heaven beyond. The conflicts in Canaan should have warned us against this view; but the whole book of Joshua, and references in the epistle to Hebrews, make it clear that the spiritual application of this story relates to the purpose of God for His people in this life: to an experience here and now of spiritual rest by victorious conflict. To such a life as this we are called. The word of God to each of us is what it was to Abram long ago, 'Get thee out . . . into . . .' and the promise made to the patriarch is made to us also, 'I will bless thee, and thou shalt be a blessing.'

Following on this divine revelation comes *a momentous resolution*: 'They went forth to go into the land of Canaan'. Here we see the importance of having a definite end in view; and it is such definiteness which makes the difference between a traveller and a tramp, between a pilgrim and a wanderer. The tramp, the wanderer, has no clear objective. It is always sheer accident that at any given time he is here or there. He does not guide his feet, but they guide him. But it is otherwise with the traveller, with the pilgrim, who — although he may not, and indeed cannot, see the path he is to tread — knows nevertheless the end for which he is making.

The two things which Abram was sure of were the starting-point, and the goal: Chaldea at the one end, and Canaan at the other. But the way between was hidden from his view. When God called him and his company to leave Ur, He said nothing to them of the path between the starting-point and the goal. That was hidden from their view, so that they went out 'not knowing whither they went'.

This is always so in the experience of the pilgrim. The main points in every life are its direction and its attainment. There are —

> Two points in the adventure of the diver,
> One — when, a beggar, he prepares to plunge,
> One — when, a prince, he rises with his pearl.

What matters it if we see not the way, so long as we are sure that we are in the right path, and know with whom we are going? We are all so anxious to know what the journey will be like, but we are called to 'walk by faith, not by sight'. The true pilgrim attitude is —

> So long Thy power hath blest me, sure it still
>   Will lead me on
> O'er moor and fen, o'er crag and torrent, till
>   The night is gone . . .
> Keep Thou my feet; I do not ask to see
> The distant scene: one step enough for me.

The Christian life is never represented as a picnic, but as something strenuous: a race, a contest, a fight, a journey with a cross. The promise of a soft life would appeal to very few, for such a life could not be productive of nobility and heroism; it would only make invalids, not men and women. To all who long for a true life, Christ is still saying, 'Get out . . . and go in . . .'

But if this is to be done, we shall have to exercise strong deter-

mination; for much of the journey to the goal will be hard and
hazardous, and only the will to continue steadfast will bring us
victoriously to the end. There are certain things of which they should
be warned who are contemplating this journey. One of these is *the
natural tendency to court delay*. After leaving Ur of the Chaldees,
Terah, Abram, and the others went several miles north-west to
Haran; and we are told they 'dwelt there'. One of the chief menaces
to the Christian life is this disposition to postpone, to procrastinate,
to dawdle on the way; and we foolishly imagine that the error is
largely compensated for by the good intention to go on to the end.
But every evil way is paved with good intentions, and by delay risks
are run which the Christian cannot afford to take. No doubt these
travellers found Haran an attractive place, surrounded by mountains, watered by rivers, and rich in pasturage. It is the place to
which Jacob went when he fled from Esau, and from that story we
learn how rich in pasture land it was, besides being a place of
commercial importance. Such resting-places are provided for
pilgrims; but it is perilous to make them dwelling-places.

Another danger of which we should be aware is *the constant
temptation to shirk difficulties*. Haran was the most northerly point
which these travellers could reach, and the time had come for them
to turn west toward the promised land. But between them and
Canaan was the broad, deep, and rapid Euphrates, which would
have to be crossed; and such a step would mean an irrevocable
cutting loose from the past life. The journey from Ur to Haran was
made on the eastern side of the river, and the feeling of entire
separation had not been felt; but now a crisis had arisen.

To such crises multitudes are not strangers. There come times in
the life of the Christian when he is confronted with problems which
are new and startling, times when momentous choices have to be
made, times when he is conscious of conflicting influences and ideals.
One voice says, 'Go forward'; another voice says, 'Stay where you
are'. Such a time as this is very critical, for the issues are of the
utmost importance.

In the story before us, Terah made one choice, and Abram made
another. They all set out from Ur to go into the land of Canaan, and
they all tarried at Haran, but Terah got no further. He died there,
and after his death Abram went on into Canaan.

This warns us of the possible tragedy of *losing desire*. The path of
the life of multitudes is littered with purposes unfulfilled, with
resolutions unredeemed. Everyone at conversion purposes to go into
the land of Canaan—that is, to enter into God's best for them. But,

alas, there are plenty of Christians who, when they see the
threatening river in front of them, and 'realize how completely the
other side of it is separated from all that is familiar, take another
thought, and conclude that they have come far enough, and that
Haran will serve their turn'. Of such was Solomon, whose 'heart was
turned from the Lord God of Israel, who had appeared unto him
twice', and of such was Demas, who forsook Paul, 'having loved this
present world'. And of such are all who are half-hearted and faint-
hearted; who will not step out until they can see the path clearly; who
drop the wider scheme of life when they see that a narrower one will
serve their purpose. But let it be clearly understood that Haran must
be abandoned if Canaan is to be reached. For earthly gains men
make great sacrifices; yet too many Christians think that they can
reach high ends without sacrificing lower and rival aims. But if we
are to run the race that is set before us, we must lay aside every
weight, and the easily besetting sin, and follow at the heels of Christ.

That brings us to the third point in our text: *a joyful realization*.
Many begin the journey, but few finish it. This, however, should be
known, that 'the Christian life is the only one which has no failures,
no balked efforts, no frustrated aims, no brave settings out and
defeated returnings'. Abram and his company set out to go into the
land of Canaan, and 'into the land of Canaan they came'.

For us, as for Abram, the secret of entering in is glad submission to
the divine will. This means separation from much to which we
naturally cling. For Abram it was from his country, his kindred, and
his father's house; and though it may not mean this for us, yet it will
mean submission and separation. Christ still says, 'Come ye out and
be separate; touch not the unclean thing, and I will receive you.'

Prompt obedience to the divine word is also a condition of entering
in, such obedience as Abram yielded when he 'went out not
knowing whither he went'. Prompt obedience is an unbending
condition of entrance into the land of rest and victory. And this
submission and obedience will lead necessarily to complete confidence in the divine wisdom, to unquestioning trust that what God
has provided for us is absolutely the best thing for us.

One further word. The reward of entering will be three-fold. There
will be *intimate fellowship with God*. Abram was called 'the friend
of God'. All Christians are God's children, but not all are God's
friends. Christ said, 'Ye are my friends if ye do whatsoever I command you.' All human friendships are based on mutual respect and
understanding, but friendship with God is based on obedience.
Another part of the reward of entering in will be *increasing fruit-*

fulness in one's own soul. Abram's spiritual growth is clearly traceable until his faith is perfected on Mount Moriah; and everyone who enters into the life of rest and victory in Christ will speedily grow in grace, and in the knowledge of things divine. And another result of this experience will be *inexhaustible fullness for others.* How great a blessing Abraham has been made to the whole world, just because he was 'the Hebrew', which means, 'the man from the other side'. We cannot be made much of a blessing to anyone so long as we are on the wrong side of the river; but if we go over to the other side, if we become true Hebrews, we shall always have an overflow to meet the need of others.

The revelation is clear, and the resolution may have been made; but have we realized it, has our purpose been accomplished, have our aspirations materialized? If not yet, why not now? Let us say to Him who is nearer to us than our breath, 'Lord, I will follow Thee whithersoever Thou goest.'

AIDEN WILSON TOZER (1897-1963)

America's contribution to evangelical spiritual writings is increasingly extensive, and in recent years no author has exercised a more potent influence, on both sides of the Atlantic, than Dr A. W. Tozer. Converted in his late teens, he joined an Alliance Church (associated with the Christian and Missionary Alliance) in 1916, married in 1918, and in 1919 became lay pastor of a church in Nutter Fort, W. Virginia. After ordination in 1920 he served three churches, successively, until 1928, when he was called to the Alliance Church in Chicago, where he exercised an influential ministry for 31 years, and became a leading personality in the C. & M.A. In 1950 he was elected editor of the *Alliance Weekly* (changed in 1958 to the *Alliance Witness*), and for 13 years his editorials commanded wide attention, in Britain as well as America. From 1959 until his sudden death in 1963 he was 'preaching minister' of Avenue Road Church, Toronto, Canada. Over a period of 20 years he produced a number of books which extended his influence far beyond that of his spoken ministry. Among these, *The Divine Conquest* (1950) was reckoned by many to be his best; its final chapter is characteristic of his forthright style.

THE SPIRIT-FILLED LIFE

That every Christian can and should be filled with the Holy Spirit would hardly seem to be a matter for debate among Christians. Yet some will argue that the Holy Spirit is not for plain Christians but for ministers and missionaries only. Others hold that the measure of the Spirit received at regeneration is identical with that received by the disciples at Pentecost and any hope of additional fullness after conversion simply rests upon error. A few will express a languid hope that some day they may be filled, and still others will avoid the subject as one about which they know very little and which can only cause embarrassment.

I want here boldly to assert that it is my happy belief that every Christian can have a copious outpouring of the Holy Spirit in a measure far beyond that they received at conversion, and I might also say, far beyond that enjoyed by the rank and file of orthodox believers today. It is important that we get this straight, for until doubts are removed faith is impossible. God will not surprise a doubting heart with an effusion of the Holy Spirit, nor will He fill anyone who has doctrinal questions about the possibility of being filled.

To remove doubts and create a confident expectation I recommend a reverent study of the Word of God itself. I am willing to rest my case upon the teachings of the New Testament. If a careful and humble examination of the words of Christ and His apostles does not lead to a belief that we may be filled with the Holy Spirit now, then I see no reason to look elsewhere. For it matters little what this or that religious teacher has said for or against the proposition. If the doctrine is not taught in the Scriptures then it cannot be supported by any argument, and all exhortations to be filled are valueless.

I shall not here present a case for the affirmative. Let the inquirer examine the evidence for himself, and if he decides that there is no warrant in the New Testament for believing that he can be filled with the Spirit, let him save himself the trouble of reading further. What I say from here on is addressed to men and women who have gotten over their questions and are confident that when they meet the conditions they may indeed be filled with the Holy Spirit.

Before a man can be filled with the Spirit *he must be sure he wants to be.* And let this be taken seriously. Many Christians want to be filled, but their desire is a vague romantic kind of thing hardly worthy to be called desire. They have almost no knowledge of what it will cost them to realize it.

Let us imagine that we are talking to an inquirer, some eager young Christian, let us say, who has sought us out to learn about the Spirit-filled life. As gently as possible, considering the pointed nature of the questions, we would probe his soul somewhat as follows: 'Are you sure you want to be filled with a Spirit who, though He is like Jesus in His gentleness and love, will nevertheless demand to be Lord of your life? Are you willing to let your personality be taken over by another, even if that other be the Spirit of God Himself? If the Spirit takes charge of your life He will expect unquestioning obedience in everything. He will not tolerate in you the self-sins even though they are permitted and excused by most Christians. By the self-sins I mean self-love, self-pity, self-seeking, self-confidence, self-righteousness, self-aggrandizement, self-defence. You will find the Spirit to be in sharp opposition to the easy ways of the world and of the mixed multitude within the precincts of religion. He will be jealous over you for good. He will not allow you to boast or swagger or show off. He will take the direction of your life away from you. He will reserve the right to test you, to discipline you, to chasten you for your soul's sake. He may strip you of many of those borderline pleasures which other Christians enjoy but which are to you a source of refined evil. Through it all He will enfold you in a love so vast, so mighty, so all-embracing, so wondrous that your very losses will seem like gains and your small pains like pleasures. Yet the flesh will whimper under His yoke and cry out against it as a burden too great to bear. And you will be permitted to enjoy the solemn privilege of suffering to "fill up that which is behind of the afflictions of Christ" in your flesh for His body's sake, which is the church. Now, with the conditions before you, do you still want to be filled with the Holy Spirit?'

If this appears severe, let us remember that the way of the cross is never easy. The shine and glamour accompanying popular religious movements is as false as the sheen on the wings of the angel of darkness when he for a moment transforms himself into an angel of light. The spiritual timidity that fears to show the cross in its true character is not on any grounds to be excused. It can result only in disappointment and tragedy at last.

Before we can be filled with the Spirit *the desire to be filled must be all-consuming.* It must be for the time the biggest thing in the life, so acute, so intrusive as to crowd out everything else. The degree of fullness in any life accords perfectly with the intensity of true desire. We have as much of God as we actually want. One great hindrance to the Spirit-filled life is the theology of complacency so widely accepted among gospel Christians today. According to this view acute desire is an evidence of unbelief and proof of lack of knowledge of the Scriptures. A sufficient refutation of this position is afforded by the Word of God itself and by the fact that it always fails to produce real saintliness among those who hold it.

Then, I doubt whether anyone ever received that divine afflatus with which we are here concerned who did not first *experience a period of deep anxiety and inward agitation*. Religious contentment is the enemy of the spiritual life always. The biographies of the saints teach that the way to spiritual greatness has always been through much suffering and inward pain. The phrase, 'the way of the cross', though it has come in certain circles to denote something very beautiful, even enjoyable, still means to the real Christian what it has always meant, the way of rejection and loss. No one ever enjoyed a cross, just as no one ever enjoyed a gallows.

The Christian who is seeking better things and who has to his consternation found himself in a state of complete self-despair need not be discouraged. Despair with self, where it is accompanied by faith, is a good friend, for it destroys one of the heart's most potent enemies and prepares the soul for the ministration of the Comforter. A sense of utter emptiness, of disappointment and darkness can (if we are alert and wise as to what is going on) be the shadow in the valley of shadows that leads on to those fruitful fields that lie further in. If we misunderstand it and resist this visitation of God we may miss entirely every benefit a kind heavenly Father has in mind for us. If we co-operate with God He will take away the natural comforts which have served us as mother and nurse for so long and put us where we can receive no help except from the Comforter Himself. He will tear away that false thing the Chinese call 'face' and show us how painfully small we really are. When He is finished with us we will know what our Lord meant when He said, 'Blessed are the poor in spirit.'

Be sure, however, that in these painful chastenings we shall not be deserted by our God. He will never leave us nor forsake us, nor will He be wroth with us nor rebuke us. He will not break His covenant nor alter that which has gone out of His mouth. He will keep us as the apple of His eye and watch over us as a mother watches over her child. His love will not fail even while He is taking us through this experience of self-crucifixion so real, so terrible, that we can express it only by crying, 'My God, my God, why hast Thou forsaken me?'

Now let us keep our theology straight about all this. There is not in this painful stripping one remote thought of human merit. The 'dark night of the soul' knows not one dim ray of the treacherous light of self-righteousness. We do not by suffering earn the anointing for which we yearn, nor does this devastation of soul make us dear to God nor give us additional favour in His eyes. The value of the stripping experience lies in its power to detach us from life's passing interests and to throw us back upon eternity. It serves to empty our earthly vessels and prepare us for the inpouring of the Holy Spirit.

The filling with the Spirit, then, requires that we give up our all, that we undergo an inward death, that we rid our hearts of the centuries-old accumulation of Adamic trash and open all rooms to the heavenly Guest.

The Holy Spirit is a living Person and should be treated as a person. We must never think of Him as a blind energy nor as an impersonal force. He hears and sees and feels as any person does. He speaks and hears us speak. We can please Him or grieve Him or silence Him as we can any other person. He will respond to our timid effort to know Him and will ever meet us over the half way.

However wonderful the crisis-experience of being filled with the Spirit, we should remember that it is only a means to something greater: that greater thing is the life-long walk in the Spirit, indwelt, directed, taught and empowered by His mighty Person. And to continue thus to walk in the Spirit requires that we meet certain conditions. These are laid down for us in the sacred Scriptures and are there for all to see.

The Spirit-filled walk demands, for instance, that we live in the Word of God as a fish lives in the sea. By this I do not mean that we study the Bible merely, nor that we take a 'course' in Bible doctrine. I mean that we should 'meditate day and night' in the sacred Word, that we should love it and feast upon it and digest it every hour of the day and night. When the business of life compels our attention we may yet, by a kind of blessed mental reflex, keep the Word of Truth ever before our minds.

Then if we would please the in-dwelling Spirit we must be all taken up with Christ. The Spirit's present work is to honour Him, and everything He does has this for its ultimate purpose. And we must make our thoughts a clean sanctuary for His holy habitation. He dwells in our thoughts, and soiled thoughts are as repugnant to Him as soiled linen to a king. Above all we must have a cheerful faith that will keep on believing however radical the fluctuation in our emotional states may be.

The Spirit in-dwelt life is not a special de luxe edition of Christianity to be enjoyed by a certain rare and privileged few who happen to be made of finer and more sensitive stuff than the rest. Rather, it is the normal state for every redeemed man and woman the world over. It is 'that mystery which hath been hid from ages and from generations, but now is made manifest to his saints: to whom God would make known what is the riches of the glory of this mystery among the gentiles: which is Christ in you, the hope of glory' (Col. 1.26). Faber, in one of his sweet and reverent hymns, addressed this good word to the Holy Spirit —

> Ocean, wide flowing Ocean, Thou,
>   Of uncreated Love;
> I tremble as within my soul
>   I feel Thy waters move.
>
> Thou art a sea without a shore;
>   Awful, immense Thou art;
> A sea which can contract itself
>   Within my narrow heart.

D. MARTYN LLOYD-JONES (1899-)

Born in South Wales, D. Martyn Lloyd-Jones trained in medicine at St Bartholomew's Hospital, London, and with the coveted degrees of MD, MRCP, seemed destined for a distinguished career as a physician. He was assistant to the eminent Lord Horder when, in 1927, he startled the medical world by abandoning medicine and returning to South Wales as minister of Sandfields Presbyterian Church, Aberavon, Port Talbot. He thus realized his early desire for the ministry, and at once became the most sought-after preacher in Wales. Chapels throughout the Principality were filled to capacity whenever he preached. In 1938 he responded to an invitation from Dr G. Campbell Morgan, who was in failing health, to become his colleague and successor-designate at Westminster Chapel, London; and there for 30 years Dr Lloyd-Jones exercised a notable ministry. His sermons on *Romans*—now being issued in volume form—are renowned throughout the English-speaking world; but it is from his earlier volumes on *The Sermon on the Mount* that the chapter on 'Adoration' is taken.

ADORATION

The second division of the Lord's Prayer deals with our petitions. 'Our Father which art in heaven': that is the invocation. Then come the petitions: 'Hallowed be Thy name. Thy kingdom come. Thy will be done in earth, as it is in heaven. Give us this day our daily bread. And forgive us our debts, as we forgive our debtors. And lead us not into temptation, but deliver us from evil.' There has been much debating among the authorities as to whether you have there six or seven petitions. The answer turns on whether that last statement 'deliver us from evil' is to be regarded as a separate petition, or whether it is to be taken as part of the previous petition and to be read like this: 'Lead us not into temptation but deliver us from evil.' It is one of those points (and there are others in connection with the Christian faith) which simply cannot be decided, and about which we cannot be dogmatic. Fortunately for us, it is not a vital point. The vital matter is to notice the order in which the petitions come. The first three—'Hallowed by Thy name. Thy kingdom come. Thy will be done on earth, as it is in heaven'—have regard to God and His glory; the others have reference to ourselves. You will notice that the first three petitions contain the word '*Thy*', and all have reference to God. It is only after that that the word '*us*' comes in: 'Give us this day our daily bread . . .' That is the vital point—the order of the petitions, not the number. The first three are concerned about and look only to God and His glory.

But let us observe something else which is of vital importance: the proportion in the petitions. Not only must our desires and petitions with regard to God come first, but we must notice, too, that half the petitions are devoted to God and His glory, and only the remainder deal with our particular needs and problems. Of course if we are interested in biblical numerics—an interest which is perhaps not to be entirely discouraged, though it can become dangerous if and when we tend to become too fanciful—we shall see, in addition, that the first *three* petitions have reference to God, and that three is always the number of Deity and of God, suggesting the three blessed Persons in the Trinity. In the same way, *four* is always the number of earth, and refers to everything that is human. There are four beasts in the heavens in the book of Revelation, and so on. Seven, which is a combination of three and four, always stands for that perfect number where we see God in His relationship to earth, and God in His dealing with men. That may be true of this prayer; our Lord may have specifically constructed it to bring out these wonderful points. We cannot prove it. But in any case the important thing to grasp is this: that it matters not what our conditions and circumstances may be, it matters not what our work may be, it matters not at all what our desires may be, we must never start with ourselves, we must never start with our own petitions.

That principle applies when our petitions reach their highest level. Even our concern for the salvation of souls, even our concern for God's blessing upon the preaching of the Word, even our concern that those who are near and dear to us may become truly Christian, even these things must never be given the first place, the first position. Still less must we ever start with our own circumstances and conditions.

It does not matter how desperate they may be, it does not matter how acute the tension, it does not matter whether it be physical illness, or war, or a calamity, or some terrible problem suddenly confronting us: whatever it may be, we must never fail to observe the order which is taught here by our blessed Lord and Saviour. Before we begin to think of ourselves and our own needs, even before our concern for others, we must start with this great concern about God and His honour and His glory. There is no principle in connection with the Christian life that exceeds this in importance. So often we err in the realm of principles. We tend to assume that we are quite sound and clear about principles, and that all we need is instruction about details. The actual truth, of course, is the exact reverse of that. If only we would always start in prayer with this true sense of the invocation; if only we were to recollect that we are in the presence of God, and that the eternal and almighty God is there, looking upon us as our Father, and more ready to bless and to surround us with His love than we are to receive His blessing, we should achieve more in that moment of recollection than all our prayers put together are likely to achieve without that realization. If only we all had this concern about God and His honour and glory.

Fortunately, our Lord knows our weakness, He realizes our need of instruction, so He has divided it up for us. He has not only announced the principle; He has divided it up for us into these three sections which we must proceed to consider. Let us look now at the first petition, 'Hallowed be Thy name.'

We realize now that we are in the presence of God, and that He is

our Father. Therefore this, says Christ, should be our first desire, our
first petition: 'Hallowed be Thy name.' What does that mean? Let us
look very briefly at the words. The word 'hallowed' means to sanctify,
or to revere, or to make and keep holy. But why does He say,
'Hallowed be Thy name'? What does this term 'Thy name' stand for?
We are familiar with the fact that it was the way in which the Jews at
that time commonly referred to God Himself. Whatever we may say
about the Jews in Old Testament times, and however great their
failures, there was one respect, at any rate, in which they were most
commendable. I refer to their sense of the greatness and the majesty
and the holiness of God. You remember that they had such a sense of
this that it had become their custom not to use the name 'Jehovah'.
They felt that the very name, the very letters, as it were, were so holy
and sacred, and they so small and unworthy, that they dare not
mention it. They referred to God as 'the Name' in order to avoid the
use of the actual term, Jehovah. So that the 'name' here means God
Himself, and we see that the purpose of the petition is to express this
desire that God Himself may be revered, may be sanctified, that the
very name of God and all it denotes and represents may be honoured
amongst men, may be holy throughout the entire world. But perhaps
in the light of the Old Testament teaching it is good for us to enlarge
on this just a little. The 'name', in other words, means all that is true
of God, and all that has been revealed concerning God. It means
God in all His attributes, God in all that He is in and of Himself, and
God in all that He has done and all that He is doing.

God, you remember, had revealed Himself to the children of Israel
under various names. He had used a term concerning Himself (*El* or
Elohim) which means His 'strength' and His 'power'; and when He
used that particular name He was giving the people a sense of His
might, His dominion, and His power. Later He revealed Himself in
that great and wonderful name *Jehovah*, which really means 'the self-
existent One', 'I am that I am', eternally self-existent. But there were
other names in which God described Himself: 'The Lord will provide'
(*Jehovah-jireh*), 'the Lord that healeth' (*Jehovah-rapha*), 'the Lord
our banner' (*Jehovah-nissi*), 'the Lord our peace' (*Jehovah-shalom*),
'the Lord our shepherd' (*Jehovah-ra-ah*), 'the Lord our
righteousness' (*Jehovah-tsidkenu*), and another term which means
'the Lord is present' (*Jehovah-shammah*). As you read the Old
Testament you will find all these various terms used; and in giving
these various names to Himself God was revealing Himself and
something of His nature and being, His character and His attributes,
to mankind. In a sense 'Thy name' stands for all that. Our Lord is

here teaching us to pray that the whole world may come to know God in this way, that the whole world may come to honour God like that. It is the expression of a burning and deep desire for the honour and glory of God.

You cannot read the four Gospels without seeing very clearly that that was the consuming passion of the Lord Jesus Christ Himself. It is found again perfectly in the great High Priestly prayer in John 17, when He says, 'I have glorified Thee on the earth,' and 'I have manifested Thy name unto the men which Thou gavest me.' He was always concerned about the glory of His Father. He said, 'I have not come to seek mine own glory but the glory of Him that sent me.' There is no real understanding of the earthly life of Christ except in these terms. He knew that glory which ever belongs to the Father, 'the glory which I had with Thee before the world was.' He had seen that glory and He had shared it. He was filled with this sense of the glory of God, and His one desire was that mankind might come to know it.

What unworthy ideas and notions this world has of God! It you test your ideas of God by the teaching of the Scriptures you will see at a glance what I mean. We lack even a due sense of the greatness and the might and the majesty of God. Listen to men arguing about God, and notice how glibly they use the term. It is not that I would advocate a return to the practice of the ancient Jews; I think they went too far. But it is indeed almost alarming to observe the way in which we all tend to use the name of God. We obviously do not realize that we are talking about the ever blessed, eternal, and absolute, almighty God. There is a sense in which we should take our shoes off our feet whenever we use the name. And how little do we appreciate the goodness of God, the kindness and the providence of God. How the Psalmist delighted in celebrating God as our rock, God as our peace, God as our shepherd who leads us, God as our righteousness, and God as the ever-present One who will never leave us nor forsake us.

This petition means just that. We should all have a consuming passion that the whole world might come to know God like that. There is an interesting expression used in the Old Testament with regard to this, which must sometimes have astonished us. The Psalmist in Psalm 34 invites everybody to join him in 'magnifying' the Lord. What a strange idea! 'O' he says, 'magnify the Lord with me, and let us exalt His name together.' At first sight that appears to be quite ridiculous. God is the eternal, the self-existent One, absolute and perfect in all His qualities. How can a feeble man ever magnify such a Being? How can we ever make God great or greater (which is what we mean by magnify)? How can we exalt the name that is highly exalted over all? It seems preposterous and quite ridiculous. And yet, of course, if we but realize the way in which the Psalmist uses it, we shall see exactly what he means. He does not mean that we can actually add to the greatness of God, for that is impossible; but he does mean that he is concerned that this greatness of God may appear to be greater amongst men. Thus it comes to pass that amongst ourselves in this world we can magnify the name of God. We can do so by words, and by our lives, by being reflectors of the greatness and the glory of God and of His glorious attributes.

That is the meaning of this petition. It means a burning desire that the whole world may bow before God in adoration, in reverence, in praise, in worship, in honour, and in thanksgiving. Is that our supreme desire? Is that the thing that is always uppermost in our minds whenever we pray to God? I would remind you again that it should be so whatever our circumstances. It is when we look at it in that way that we see how utterly valueless much of our praying must be. When you come to God, says our Lord in effect, even though you may be in desperate conditions and circumstances, it may be with some great concern on your mind and in your heart; even then, He says, stop for a moment and just recollect and realize this, that your greatest desire of all should be that this wonderful God, who has become your Father in and through me, should be honoured, should be worshipped, should be magnified amongst the people. 'Hallowed be Thy name.' And it has always been so in the praying of every true saint of God that has ever lived on the face of the earth.

If, therefore, we are anxious to know God's blessing and are concerned that our prayers should be effectual and of value, we must follow this order. It is all put in a phrase repeated many times in the Old Testament: 'The fear of the Lord is the beginning of wisdom.' That is the conclusion reached by the Psalmist. That is the conclusion, likewise, of the wise man in his proverbs. If you want to know, he says, what true wisdom is, if you want to be blessed and prosperous, if you want to have peace and joy, if you want to be able to live and die in a worthy manner, if you want wisdom with regard to life in this world, here it is: 'the fear of the Lord.' That does not mean craven fear; it means reverential awe. If, therefore, we want to know God and to be blessed of God, we must start by worshipping Him. We must say, 'Hallowed be Thy name', and tell Him that, before mentioning any concern about ourselves, our one desire is that He shall be known. Let us approach God 'with reverence and godly fear: for our God is a consuming fire'. That is the first petition.

The second is, 'Thy kingdom come'. You notice there is a logical order in these petitions. They follow one another by a kind of inevitable, divine necessity. We began by asking that the name of God may be hallowed amongst men. But the moment we pray that prayer we are reminded of the fact that His name is not hallowed thus. At once the question arises, Why do not all men bow before the sacred name? Why is not every man on this earth concerned about humbling himself now in the presence of God, and worshipping Him, and using every moment in adoring Him and spreading forth His name? Why not? The answer is, of course, because of sin, because there is another kingdom, the kingdom of Satan, the kingdom of darkness. And there at once we are reminded of the very essence of the human problems and the human predicament. Our desire as Christian people is that God's name shall be glorified. But the moment we start with that we realize that there is this opposition, and we are reminded about the whole biblical teaching about evil. There is another who is 'the god of this world'; there is a kingdom of darkness, a kingdom of evil, and it is opposed to God and His glory and honour. But God has been graciously pleased to reveal from the very dawn of history that He is yet going to establish His kingdom in this world of time, that though Satan has entered in and conquered the world for the time being, and the whole of mankind is under his dominion, He is again going to assert Himself and turn this world and all its kingdoms into His own glorious kingdom. In other words, running right through the Old Testament there are the promises and the prophecies concerning the coming of the kingdom of God, or the kingdom of heaven. And, of course, at this particular, crucial point of world history, when our Lord Himself was here on earth, this matter was very much in the forefront of men's minds. John the Baptist had been preaching his message, 'Repent ye: for the kingdom of heaven is at hand.' He called the people to be ready for it. And when our Lord began preaching, He said exactly the same thing: 'Repent: for the kingdom of heaven is at hand.' In this petition He obviously has that whole idea in His mind as He teaches His disciples to offer this particular prayer. At that immediate historical point He was teaching His disciples to pray that this kingdom of God should come increasingly and come quickly; but the prayer is equally true and equally right for us as Christian people in all ages until the end shall come.

We can summarize the teaching concerning the kingdom. The kingdom of God really means the reign of God; it means the law and the rule of God. When we look at it like that we can see that the kingdom can be regarded in three ways. In one sense the kingdom has already come. It came when the Lord Jesus Christ was here. He said, 'If I with the finger of God cast out devils, no doubt the kingdom of God is come upon you.' He said in effect, 'The kingdom of God is here now; I am exercising this power, this sovereignty, this majesty, this dominion; this is the kingdom of God.' So the kingdom of God in one sense had come then. The kingdom of God is also here at this moment in the hearts and lives of all who submit to Him, in all who believe in Him. The kingdom of God is present in the church, in the heart of all those who are truly Christian. Christ reigns in such people. But the day is yet to come when His kingdom shall have been established here upon earth. The day is yet to come when:

Jesus shall reign where'er the sun
Does his successive journeys run.

That day is coming. The whole message of the Bible looks forward to that. Christ came down from heaven to earth to found, to establish, and to bring in this kingdom. He is still engaged upon that task, and will be until the end, when it shall have been completed. Then He will, according to Paul, hand it back to God the Father, 'that God may be all in all.'

So our petition really amounts to this: We should have a great longing and desire that the kingdom of God and of Christ may come in the hearts of men. It should be our desire that this kingdom should be extended in our own hearts; for it is to the extent that we worship Him, and surrender our lives to Him, and are led by Him, that His kingdom comes in our hearts. We should also be anxious to see this kingdom extending in the lives and hearts of other men and women. So that when we pray, 'Thy kingdom come', we are praying for the success of the Gospel, its sway and power; we are praying for the conversion of men and women; we are praying that the kingdom of God may come today in Britain, in Europe, in America, in Australia, everywhere in the world. 'Thy kingdom come' is an all-inclusive missionary prayer.

But it goes even further than that. It is a prayer which indicates that we are 'looking for and hasting unto the coming of the day of God' (2 Peter 3.12). It means that we should be anticipating the day when all sin and evil and wrong, and everything that is opposed to God, shall finally have been routed. It means that we should have longings in our hearts for the time when the Lord will come back again, when all that is opposed to Him shall be cast into the lake of burning, and the kingdoms of this world shall have become the kingdoms of our God and of His Christ.

Thy kingdom come, O God;
Thy rule, O Christ, begin;
Break with Thine iron rod
The tyrannies of sin.

That is the petition. Indeed its meaning is expressed perfectly at the very end of the book of Revelation. 'Even so, come, Lord Jesus.' 'The Spirit and the bride say, Come.' Our Lord is just emphasizing here that before we begin to think of our own personal needs and desires, we should have this burning desire within us for the coming of His kingdom, that the name of God may be glorified and magnified over all.

The third petition, 'Thy will be done in earth, as it is in heaven, needs no explanation. It is a kind of logical consequence and conclusion from the second, as that was a logical conclusion from the first. The result of the coming of the kingdom of God amongst men will be that the will of God will be done amongst men. In heaven the will of God is always being done perfectly. We have only some dim and faint figures of it in the Scriptures, but we have sufficient to know that what is characteristic of heaven is that everyone and everything is waiting upon God and anxious to glorify and magnify His name. The angels, as it were, are on the wing, all ready and waiting to fly at His bidding. The supreme desire of all in heaven is to do the will of God, and thereby to praise and worship Him. And it should be the desire of every true Christian, says our Lord here, that all on earth should be the same. Here again we are looking forward to the coming of the kingdom, because this petition will never be fulfilled and granted until the kingdom of God shall indeed be established here on earth amongst men. Then the will of God will be done on earth as it is done in heaven. There will be 'new heavens and a new earth, wherein dwelleth righteousness'. Heaven and earth will become one, the world will be changed, evil will be burned out of it, and the glory of God will shine over all.

In these words, then, we are taught how we begin to pray. Those are the petitions with which we must always start. We can summarize them again in this way: Our innermost and greatest desire should be the desire for God's honour and glory. At the risk of being misunderstood I suggest that our desire for this should be even greater than our desire for the salvation of souls. Before we even begin to pray for souls, before we even begin to pray for the extension and spread of God's kingdom, there should be that over-ruling desire for the manifestation of the glory of God, and that all might humble themselves in His presence. We can put it like this. What is it that troubles and worries our minds? Is it the manifestation of sin that we see in the world, or is it the fact that men do not worship and glorify God as they ought to do? Our Lord felt it so much that He put it like this in John 17: 'O righteous Father, the world hath not known Thee: but I have known Thee, and these (referring to the disciples) have known that Thou hast sent me.' 'Righteous Father', He said in effect, 'here is the tragedy, here is the thing that perplexes me and saddens me, that the world has not known Thee. It thinks of Thee as a tyrant, it thinks of Thee as a harsh law-giver, it thinks of Thee as someone who is opposed to it, and always tyrannizing over it. Holy Father, the world has not known Thee. If it had but known Thee it could never think of Thee like that.' And that should be our attitude, that should be our burning desire and longing. We should so know God that our one longing and desire should be that the whole world should come to know Him too.

What a wonderful prayer this is. Oh, the folly of people who say that such a prayer is not meant for Christians, but that it was meant only for the disciples then and for the Jews in some coming age. Does it not make us feel in a sense that we have never prayed at all? This is prayer. 'Our Father which art in heaven, Hallowed by Thy name.' Have we arrived at that yet, I wonder? Have we really prayed that prayer, that petition, 'Hallowed be Thy name?' If only we are right about that, the rest will follow. 'Thy kingdom come. Thy will be done in earth, as it is in heaven.' We need not turn to Him and ask Him, 'Lord, teach us to pray.' He has done so already. We have but to put into practice the principles He has taught us so plainly in this model prayer.

GEORGE B. DUNCAN (1912—   )

The son of Church of Scotland missionaries, George B. Duncan was born in India and educated in Edinburgh — at Merchiston Castle School and the University. After graduating he became the representative in Scotland of the Children's Special Service Mission (later re-named the Scripture Union), and initiated the work of SU in Scotland's secondary schools. Preparation for the Anglican ministry followed, at Bristol, and he served a three years' curacy at Broadwater Church, Worthing. During incumbencies in Carlisle, Edinburgh and Cockfosters — a suburb of Greater London — George Duncan became widely known as a Convention speaker. Returning to the church of his fathers, he was minister of Portland Church, Troon, for six years; and then for twelve years at the important Glasgow city church of St George's Tron, until his retirement in 1977. He had for several years paid visits to Conventions in various parts of the world, and now devotes all his time to this wider itinerant ministry. His address on 'the old prophet' at the Keswick Convention in 1956 held the vast congregation in almost breathless silence, and is remembered as one of the most impressive occasions in the Convention's recent history.

A PERIL OF SPIRITUAL MATURITY

I want to consider with you some aspects of failure in Christian living which are peculiarly the peril of those who have grown older in Christian experience, and to do so against the background of the story recorded in 1 Kings 13; and if we want a text to focus our thought, we shall take it from v. 11, 'Now there dwelt an old prophet in Bethel . . .'

May I begin by saying that *age has its prerogatives*. There are some things that age has that youth can never have. I think, for instance, of the *wealth of experience* that age alone can enjoy. I suppose that most of us know what it is to meet older Christians who are rich in experience, who have a wealth of memory that makes them seem rich indeed; veterans of many battlefields and conquests; men and women who have walked a long way with God. They have a maturity of judgement, a knowledge of life and of the Bible, a knowledge of God, that seem to make the problems that baffle and perplex us quite simple, and enable them to avoid the mistakes that those of us who are younger so easily make. In this wealth of experience they have a prerogative over youth; and also, I believe, in *the work of encouragement*. Many of us can recall meeting Christians the wealth of whose experience has humbled us, for they have accomplished a work of encouragement which has helped us along. And how humbly grateful we shall ever be for that ministry and that memory, that set our feet steadfastly on the way.

But while age and experience have their prerogatives, they have also their *perils*; and it is to these I want to turn your thought.

Years ago I heard a Christian say, 'Few Christians end well.' If that is true, then it is more than ever vital that the experienced Christian who so rightly thinks that 'he standeth', should 'take heed lest he fall'. Let us turn, then, and look into the mirror of God's Word and see there *ourselves*; and as we read I want to remind you that age is a relative term, and God's Word may come to those who are not so very old, but older than others. So let us look at this old prophet who dwelt in Bethel. And first I want to note with you what I call —
THE LETHARGY THAT MARKED HIS SERVICE.

Here was a man who had spiritually very nearly come to a stand-still. Note *the inaction into which he had settled down*. Bethel, where he lived, was the scene of Jeroboam's sin — the setting up of a false religion, served by false priests. The details are found in the closing verses of the previous chapter. The action of the king was to become proverbial and legendary in the history of Israel: Jeroboam was the king 'who made Israel to sin'.

The motive of Jeroboam's sin was political expediency; the action one of spiritual apostasy. And in the face of this challenge, the old prophet was silent. He had nothing to say, and said nothing. I wonder why. Why had this lethargy settled down across his service for God? I wonder if it was because of *weariness*. He had fought through many battles in the past: he just could not rouse himself for yet another battle; this time he would leave it to others to fight. Or perhaps it was *wordly wisdom* — for he had a family to look after, and it would not do to incur disfavour in high places. Would it matter if he compromised just this once, and let this thing pass unrebuked?

Whatever the reasons why, the silence remained unbroken, the message unspoken, and the servant of God remained at home. The lethargy that marked his service.

I want to ask, 'Is your pace slowing down? Spiritually, vitally, have you very nearly come to a halt and a standstill? There was a time when no one was keener than you in the ministry of prayer. In your own prayer life you prayed with some purpose. In the prayer life of your church you could always be relied upon; your prayer meant so much to the church, to God, to the minister, to yourself. But in your praying you have slowed down; and for weeks, for months, it may be for years, 'the old prophet' has come almost to a halt in his prayer life.

In your consecration you were once fastidiously careful; your standards were high, almost intolerably so, in your separation to Christ from the world: but it cost so much to maintain that standard, and you grew so weary, and so 'wise', that slowly and almost imperceptibly the world has encroached, and as far as consecration is concerned, you have almost forgotten the meaning of the word.

What about your service? How desperately keen you were; how unashamedly you used to go out for the conversion of others — and you saw them converted. But that has all stopped now; you are not interested in that; you do not toil for that; you do not labour for that; you do not preach for that; you do not suffer for that as once you did. You are a Christian still, you are a prophet still; you still hold office — you are a deacon, an elder, a Sunday-school teacher, a member of committee, a minister, a bishop, a missionary, a Christian parent; you are holding office. Yet all the spiritual vitality has been drained out of it, and there is a lethargy upon your service, and you have come to a halt, you are at a standstill. Your testimony? You have none. Your usefulness has practically gone. You are holding on to a position; you have a rank to which you have ceased to have the spiritual right. The inaction into which he had settled.

Then notice *the intrusion by which he was startled*. The lethargy which was upon the life of this old prophet was suddenly, rudely startled; the silence which he had been careful to maintain was suddenly, sharply broken. His sons rushed in to tell him of the dramatic event: that the king himself had been officiating at the high place that very day, and the man of God, a young man of Judah, had dramatically interrupted the service. The curse of God had been pronounced against the altar; and the king, violently angry, had caused the instant arrest of the man of God — and he had been struck immediately by the hand of God in judgement. Then, a cowed and frightened king had pleaded for mercy, before a rent altar, amid the smoke of the scattered ashes. A cringing and conciliatory monarch had offered hospitality and rewards — to find his offer treated with contempt. What had been the words of the man of God from Judah, to the king? 'If thou wilt give me half thine house, I will not go in with thee, neither will I eat bread nor drink water in this place: for so was it charged me by the word of the Lord.' The long silence had been broken, and like a sudden peal of thunder out of a leaden and sullen sky, the voice of God had spoken; and with glowing faces the sons of the old prophet ended their breathless story, while the old man watched and listened.

What was it that turned their glowing faces into puzzled wonderment? Was it the sudden, stabbing realization that what had just happened should have happened long ago? And that the man who should have done it was not the man of God from Judah, but the old prophet, their father, to whom they now told their story — across whose face consternation and anger now chased each other, until finally a burning, sullen anger settled there, and the man who had been inactive so long, stung into action, demanded, 'Where did the man of God go?'

The intrusion by which he was startled. All I know is this, that again and again where the lethargy of our service has slowed down to inaction, that when an intrusion comes to startle us into amazement and into anger — when a minister comes to the church with a flaming heart; a son or a daughter is converted in their Christian home to God, and with passionate devotion they give their all to Christ; when a man or a girl joins the fellowship of the church with heart afire for

God; a Christian comes into the office, a new nurse starts her training in the hospital, a new curate joins the staff.—and the silence is broken. The lethargy is startled into alarm. God begins to speak directly, where there was a comfortable security and quietness. All is disturbed and confused. And the 'old prophet', amazed, alarmed, angry, is stirred to action at last.

The lethargy that marked his service. . . . Is there an old prophet here? Spiritually you have come to a halt. Has somebody come into your life? Has the voice of God spoken? Worse followed, for the lethargy that marked the service of the old prophet was replaced by what I call—

THE ANIMOSITY THAT SEARED HIS SPIRIT

Here we face the tragic fact that the man who took no action at all against the deeds of Jeroboam, became passionately and angrily active against the man of God. One of the things that appals me, that shames me, is just this very thing: the ceaseless animosity of Christian against Christian. You find it in churches, in fellowships, on mission stations, in societies; you find it wherever you find Christians: and the tragedy is that those involved are very seldom youngsters in the faith. Children do not normally kill children. Men kill men. You do not find it in the Sunday-school, you do not find it among the young people in the youth fellowship; you do not find it among the confirmation candidates. You find it at a higher level. You find it among the older Christians, in your deacons' court, among your elders, in your kirk session; you find it among your clergy and ministers, in your committees, among your Sunday-school teachers, in Christian parents; you find it in 'the old prophet'. That is where you find it, the animosity that sears the spirit. Then you find that those who have ceased to be active in the vital things of God against the enemy of souls, are tirelessly active against the 'men of God'. Why? Why was this old prophet roused to action—not against the false worship of Jeroboam: he did not do a thing about that. Why was he roused to action against the faithful servant of Jehovah?

I think, first of all, because of *a pride that would not be humbled*. The man's pride was hurt to the quick. The man who remained unmoved when God's name was dishonoured, was stung to the quick when his own actions were condemned. The security and comfort he had gained by compromising his loyalty had been treated with contempt by another. The standard that he had lowered by his slackness had been raised again to the mast by the zealousness of the man of God. The silence he had so carefully maintained had been broken. The message he had ceased to declare had been declared by another. Everything he knew he should have been, and had failed to be, the man of God from Judah had been. And as his own sons told the story of it all, they told the story of his own condemnation; and his pride hated it. A man in his position, a man of his age, a man of his experience, being condemned, being judged! He had been weighed in the balance and found wanting. Not explicitly, for the man of God from Judah had not said a word about him; but he had been condemned implicitly. He sensed it as he listened to the story told by his own sons. He saw it in the glow that had been kindled, and still glowed, on their faces. His imagination ran riot as he followed the telling of the story in a thousand homes in Bethel that day; and with the telling he would have been called 'the old prophet, the man who had done nothing, the man who had lowered•his standards, the man who had compromised . . .' Condemned, condemned . . . and *he hated it*.

Have you a pride that will not be humbled? Oh, his wounded, resentful pride writhed and twisted with the pain of it all, until the focus of all the hate and all the hurt was found in *a purpose that would not be halted*—to find the man, and somehow to bring him down: to bring him down to his own level, and to make him swallow those words of contempt, 'neither will I eat bread nor drink water in this place', making himself out to be better than the old prophet— for *he* had been eating bread and drinking water there for these years and months past. So the purpose was formulated and pursued until he found the man of God. The animosity that seared his spirit.

Tell me, are you more active against the people of God than against the enemies of God? Is it possible? Do you write more, do you talk more, do you think more, do you plan more, against the servants of God, than His enemies? Do you? I'll tell you why. Because the life of somebody has condemned you. Not verbally, but implicitly. Am I speaking to some parents, whose child's love for Jesus Christ condemns your lack of love? Am I speaking to some minister, and the zeal of someone in your church condemns your lack of it? Am I speaking to some Christian worker, and your compromising with the world is condemned by the consecration of your colleague: some clerk or typist, some nurse, and your silence is condemned by the witness of that new girl; some missionary, and the standard of your devotion to Jesus Christ—or lack of it—is condemned by another? Tell me, have you got a pride that will not be humbled? Are you in your heart pursuing some devilish purpose to bring that one down by fair means or foul, that they too may come under condemnation for having dared to suggest that you, with your position, with all your experience, and of your age, that *you* were wrong?

We have been looking into the mirror of God's truth in the light of this 'old prophet', and we have seen the lethargy that marked his service, the animosity that seared his spirit; note finally —

THE TRAGEDY THAT CROWNED HIS SUCCESS

For the old prophet succeeded. And you too can succeed. Parent, you can take the love of your child for Christ, that love, that burden for souls; and *you can kill that*. Brother minister, you can temper all the burning zeal of that young fellow, and quench it. Christian worker, you can lower the standards of that other young person, you can silence that fresh and artless testimony. You can. The old prophet did. And to do it, you will use *the weapon that he used*. Do you know what it was? He used his tongue. And with a blend of friendliness, a touch of authority, a suggestion of divine guidance, with his tongue the old prophet *lied*.

And as he spoke, he knew that he lied. You, too, can use your tongue — one of the most powerful and deadly things we possess. That is why it is one of the touchstones of Christian maturity. 'If any man offend not in word (in tongue) the same is a perfect man.' You can go on talking persistently; you can speak authoritatively; you can even use the language of spirituality: and in the use of your tongue *you can lie*. And even as you are claiming that what you say is right, you know in your heart that you are lying.

The old prophet knew that he lied. Older Christian, in your dealings with the young, with that other servant of God — whether flagrantly, whether obviously, or whether rather cleverly and with just a tinge of suggestion — you are a liar, and you know it. The weapon you used was the weapon the old prophet used. It was the weapon the devil used when he said to our first parents, 'Ye shall not surely die!'

The weapon he used; and *the wreckage he saw* . . . for he brought the young man to the path of disobedience. He brought him into the path of danger. He brought him to the place of death. For suddenly a leap from the lion, a moment of agony, and a life of usefulness was over. The tragedy that crowned his success.

You see, he did succeed. And one of the supreme tragedies of age is that when we succeed, *we kill* . . . somebody's love for the Master, somebody's purpose of obedience, somebody's devotion and surrender. We succeed, and we slay.

Old prophet, how many lives of usefulness have you ended? The life of one of your children? A member of your church? Somebody on the mission station? Somebody who came under your authority? You lied, and you slew. Old prophet, is there somebody you have not killed yet, but are planning to? Come, stand for just one moment by the wreckage of the life you lied to destroy. Can you see the face, as the old prophet looked on the face of the man of God on the road that day. The love you killed, the devotion you slew, the testimony you silenced, the consecration you destroyed, the usefulness you ended.

Come, stand by the old prophet. I wonder if you have one thing more in common with him. Can you share this—*the agony that broke his heart*? 'And the old prophet came to the city to mourn . . .'

If you don't know what it is to weep here, I only hope that God will give you a place in heaven where you can weep, and weep, and weep, and weep . . . for the child of God whose usefulness you killed, whose love you extinguished. Ah, there are those alive today, but all the testimony, all the usefulness, everything worthwhile is *dead*. And it was an old prophet who did it.

JOHN R. W. STOTT (1921 -   )

The acknowledged leader of Anglican Conservative Evangelicals, John R. W. Stott is the son of a distinguished physician, Sir Arnold Stott, KBE. He went from Rugby School to Trinity College, Cambridge, where he read modern languages and theology. Ordained in 1945, he served as curate at the well-known church of All Souls, Langham Place, in the heart of London's West End, where after a time he was called upon to carry full responsibility for the services during the incumbent's long illness; consequently in 1950 he was appointed rector of the church. Steadily expanding attendances necessitated the relaying of services to 'overflow' congregations in the nearby 'daughter' church of St Peter's, Vere Street. In 1959 Mr Stott was appointed a chaplain to the Queen. The increasing demands of engagements abroad led to his resignation as rector in 1975, but continuing relationship to All Souls as rector-emeritus. The author of several books, he himself indicated the final chapter of *Christ the Controversialist* for reproduction in this volume.

JESUS, TEACHER AND LORD

George Ingle, late Bishop of Willesden, once wrote about 'the sad situation of a divided church' and about the even sadder spectacle of 'division . . . within the same church'. He continued, 'Allegiance to *a* church, or even to a party within that church, comes before allegiance to Christ' (*The Lord's Creed*, Collins). If I thought that being an evangelical Christian involved a party loyalty which took precedence over allegiance to Christ, I would give up being an evangelical immediately. The very idea of subordinating Christ to a party is abhorrent to me. The evangelical's sincerely held belief is that his very loyalty to Christ requires him to hold evangelical views. (Every evangelical could echo Charles Simeon's statement of his own position: 'As for names and parties in religion, he equally disclaims them all; he takes his religion from the Bible, and endeavours, as much as possible, to speak as that speaks'.)

In the major controversies of Christ with the Pharisees and Sadducees, He attributed the Sadducees' error to their ignorance of the power of God. In contrast to the Pharisees He insisted that our authority is to be found in God's Word alone without the addition of human traditions, and our acceptance in God's mercy alone without the addition of human merits. He taught that the morality and the worship pleasing to God are those of the heart, inward rather than outward. He emphasized that our Christian responsibility is to be involved in the world, not to withdraw from it, and that our overriding Christian ambition should not be to seek our own glory, but the glory of God.

These issues emerge plainly from the debates of Jesus with the religious leaders of His day. And each debate has continued into our own day. Not one of them is dead. The only question is whether we range ourselves with Him or with those He criticized; whether our Christianity is in fact Christian or a modern version of Pharisaism or Sadduceeism.

In this connection I have myself been helped by some words Jesus spoke in the Upper Room just after He had washed the apostles' feet. When He had resumed His place He said to them, 'You call me Teacher and Lord; and you are right, for so I am. If I then, your Lord and Teacher, have washed your feet, you also ought to wash one another's feet' (John 13. 13–14). Now 'Teacher' and 'Lord' were polite forms of address used in conversation with rabbis. And the apostles used them in addressing Jesus. What He was now saying is that in His case they were more than courtesy titles; they expressed a fundamental reality. As the New English Bible renders it, 'You call me Teacher and Lord, and rightly so, for that is what I am.' I am in fact, He declared, what you call me in title.

This verse tells us something of great importance both about Christ and about Christians.

What it tells us about Christ concerns His divine self-consciousness. Though but a peasant from Galilee, carpenter by trade and preacher by vocation, He claimed to be the teacher and the lord of men. He said He had authority over them to tell them what to believe and to do. It is an evident (if indirect) claim to deity, for no mere man can ever exercise lordship over other men's minds and wills. Moreover, in advancing His claim He showed no sign of mental unbalance. On the contrary, He had just risen from supper, girded Himself with a towel, poured water into a basin, got on His hands and knees, and washed their feet. He who said He was their teacher and lord humbled Himself to be their servant. And it is this paradoxical combination of lordship and service, authority and humility, lofty claims and lowly conduct, which constitutes the strongest evidence that (in John's words in this passage) 'He had come from God and was going to God' (v.3).

Secondly, the same verse reveals the proper relationship of Christians to Christ. This is not only that of a sinner to his Saviour, but also of a pupil to his Teacher and of a servant to his Lord. Indeed, these things belong indissolubly together. He is 'our Lord and Saviour Jesus Christ' (This full title occurs several times in the New Testament. See, *e.g.*, 2 Pet. 1.11; 3.18). What, then, are the implications of acknowledging Jesus as Teacher and Lord?

Of course everybody agrees that Jesus of Nazareth was a great teacher, and many are prepared to go at least as far as Nicodemus and call Him 'a teacher come from God' (John 3.2). Further, it is clear that one of the most striking characteristics of His teaching was the authority with which He gave it. He did not hum and haw and hesitate. Nor did He ever speak tentatively, diffidently, apologetically. No. He knew what He wanted to say, and He said it with quiet, simple dogmatism. It is this that impressed people so much. As they listened to Him, we read, 'they were astonished at His teaching, for His word was with authority'.

There is only one logical deduction from these things. If the Jesus who thus taught with authority was the Son of God made flesh, we must bow to His authority and accept His teaching. We must allow our opinions to be moulded by His opinions, our views to be conditioned by His views. And this includes His uncomfortable and unfashionable teaching, like His view of God as a supreme, spiritual, personal, powerful Being, the Creator, Controller, Father and King; and of man as a created being, made in the image of God but now fallen, with a heart so corrupt as to be the source of all the evil things he thinks, says and does. Again, He taught the divine origin, supreme authority and complete sufficiency of Scripture as God's Word written, whose primary purpose is to direct the sinner to his Saviour in order to find life. He also taught the fact of divine judgement as a process of sifting which begins in this life and is settled at death. He confirmed that the final destinies of men are the awful alternatives of heaven and hell, adding that these destinies are irrevocable with a great gulf fixed between them.

Yet these traditional Christian truths are being called in question today. The independent, personal, transcendent being of God; the radical sinfulness of man; the inspiration and authority of Scripture; the solemn, eternal realities of heaven and hell — all this (and more) is being not only questioned but in many places actually abandoned. Our simple contention is that no one can jettison such plain gospel truths as these and still call Jesus 'Teacher'.

There have been other religious teachers, even if less authoritative than Jesus. But Jesus went further, claiming also to be Lord. A teacher will instruct his pupils. He may even plead with them to follow his teaching. He cannot command assent, however, still less obedience. Yet this prerogative was exercised by Jesus as Lord. 'If you love me,' He said, 'you will keep my commandments.' 'He who loves father or mother . . . son or daughter more than me is not worthy of me' (John 14.15; Matt. 10.37). He asked from His disciples nothing less than their supreme love and loyalty.

So Christians look to Jesus Christ as both their Teacher and their Lord; their Teacher to instruct them and their Lord to command them. We are proud to be more than His pupils; we are His servants as well. We recognize His right to lay upon us duties and obligations: 'If I then, your Lord and Teacher, have washed your feet, you also *ought* to wash one another's feet.' This 'ought' we accept from the authority of Jesus. We desire not only to submit our minds to His teaching but our wills to His obedience. And this is what He expected: 'Truly, truly, I say to you, a servant (literally, slave) is not greater than his master' (John 13.16). He therefore calls us to adopt

His standards, which are totally at variance with the world's, and to measure greatness in terms not of success but of service, not of self-aggrandisement but of self-sacrifice.

Because we are fallen and proud human beings, we find this part of Christian discipleship very difficult. We like to have our own opinions (especially if they are different from everybody else's) and to air them rather pompously in conversation. We also like to live our own lives, set our own standards, and go our own way. In brief, we like to be our own master, our own teacher and lord. People sometimes defend this position by saying that it would be impossible, and if it were possible it would be wrong, to surrender our independence of thought. Charlie Watts of the Rolling Stones beat group expressed this view when he said: 'I'm against any form of organized thought. I'm against . . . organized religion like the church. I don't see how you can organize 10,000,000 minds to believe one thing' (reported in *The Guardian*, 19 October 1967). This is the mood of the day, both in the world and in the church. It is a self-assertive and anti-authoritarian mood. It is not prepared either to believe or to do anything simply because some 'authority' requires it. But what if that authority is Christ's, and if Christ's authority is God's? What then? The only Christian answer is that we submit, humbly, gladly, and with the full consent of our mind and will.

But do we? Is this in fact our regular practice? It is quite easy to put ourselves to the test. What is our authority for believing what we believe and doing what we do? Is it in reality what we think and what we want? Or is it what Professor So-and-so has written, what Bishop Such-and-such has said? Or is it what Jesus Christ has made known, either Himself directly or through His apostles?

We may not particularly like what He taught about God and man, Scripture and salvation, worship and morality, duty and destiny, heaven and hell. But are we daring to prefer our own opinions and standards to His, *and still call ourselves Christian*? Or are we presuming to say that He did not know what He was talking about, that He was a weak and fallible teacher, or even accommodated Himself to the views of His contemporaries although He knew them to be mistaken? Such suggestions are dreadfully derogatory to the honour of the Son of God.

Of course we have a responsibility to grapple with Christ's teaching, its perplexities and problems, endeavouring to understand it and to relate it to our own situation. But ultimately the question before the church can be simply stated: Is Jesus Christ Lord or not? And if He is Lord, is He Lord of all? The Lordship of Jesus must be

allowed to extend over every part of those who have confessed that
'Jesus is Lord', including their minds and their wills. Why should
these be exempt from His otherwise universal dominion? No-one is
truly converted who is not intellectually and morally converted. No-
one is intellectually converted if he has not submitted his mind to the
mind of the Lord Christ, nor morally converted if he has not submitted his will to the will of the Lord Christ.

Further, such submission is not bondage but freedom. Or rather,
it is that kind of willing Christian bondage which is perfect Christian
freedom — freedom from the vagaries of self and from the fashions of
the world (and of the church), freedom from the shifting sands of
subjectivity, freedom to exercise our minds and our wills as God
intended them to be exercised, not in rebellion against Him but in
submission to Him.

I do not hesitate to say that Jesus Christ is looking for men and
women in the church of this kind and calibre today, who will take
Him seriously as their Teacher and Lord, not paying lip-service to
these titles ('Why do you call me "Lord, Lord," and not do what I tell
you?'), but actually taking His yoke upon them, in order to learn
from Him and to 'take every thought captive to obey Christ' (Luke
6.46; Matt. 11.29–30; 2 Cor. 10.5).

This will involve for us, first, a greater diligence in study. We can
neither believe or obey Jesus Christ if we do not know what He taught.
One of the most urgent needs of the contemporary church is a far
closer acquaintance with Scripture among ordinary church members. How lovingly the pupil should cherish the teaching of such a
Master!

It will also involve a greater humility in subordination. By nature
we hate authority and love independence. We think it a great thing
to have an independent judgment and manifest an independent
spirit. And so it is if by this we mean that we do not wish to be sheep
who follow the crowd, or reeds shaken by the winds of public
opinion. But independence of Jesus Christ is not a virtue; it is a sin,
and indeed a grievous sin in one who professes to be a Christian. The
Christian is not at liberty to disagree with Christ or to disobey Christ.
On the contrary, his great concern is to conform both his mind and
his life to Christ's teaching.

And the reasonableness of this Christian subordination lies in the
identity of the Teacher. If Jesus of Nazareth were a mere man, it
would be ludicruous thus to submit our minds and our wills to Him.
But because He is the Son of God, it is ludicrous not to do so. Rather
is submission to Him just plain Christian common sense and duty.

I believe that Jesus Christ is addressing the church of our day with the same words: 'You call me Teacher and Lord; and you are right, for so I am.' My prayer is that, having listened to His words, we shall not be content with the use of these courtesy titles, but give Him due honour by our humble belief and wholehearted obedience.

INDEX